When GOD Sends an Angel

P9-BAT-785

 Publications International, Ltd.

Contributing Writers:
Nicola A'Donato: 141; Jane Edwards Aldrich: 190; Joanne Baily Baxter: 128; Patti Bierer: 33; Ross Brown: 49; Renie Szilak Burghardt: 133; Cecil Burnette: 185; Mary Chandler: 79; Elaine Creasman: 15; Joseph Curreri: 155; Christine Dallman: 84; Sharon Ervin: 71; Katherine Erwin: 120; Susan Fahncke: 176; Pat Gilbers: 151; Millie Garner Grey: 113; Bonnie Compton Hanson: 58, 65; Margaret Anne Huffman: 28, 90, 148; Ellen Javernick: 18, 40, 53, 95, 130, 172; Marie Jones: 4, 36, 45; Karen Leet: 8, 12, 180; Mary Lu Leon: 138; Therese Marszalek: 160; Wilma J. Masingale: 163; Robbie Morris as told to Frances E. Sames: 106; Barbara Morrow: 75; Kathleen Muldoon: 67; Rebecca S. Ramsey: 123; Carol McAdoo Rehme: 34, 109, 169; Susan Sage: 117; Elsie Stover Schad: 100; Carol Solstad: 60; Joyce Stark: 86; William R. Stimson: 22; Annie Wyndham: 103.

Acknowledgments:
Scripture taken from the New Revised Standard Version of the Bible, copyright © 1989, by the Division of Christian Education of the National Council of the Churches of Christ in the United States of America, and are used by permission. All rights reserved.

Copyright © 2007 Publications International, Ltd. All rights reserved. This book may not be reproduced or quoted in whole or in part by any means whatsoever without written permission from:

Louis Weber, CEO
Publications International, Ltd.
7373 North Cicero Avenue
Lincolnwood, Illinois 60712

Permission is never granted for commercial purposes.

Manufactured in U.S.A.

8 7 6 5 4 3 2 1

ISBN-13: 978-0-7853-7570-8

ISBN-10: 0-7853-7570-8

CONTENTS

4

SEND ME AN ANGEL

8

GUIDING ANGELS

45

LOVING ANGELS

75

GUARDIAN ANGELS

109

COMFORTING ANGELS

133

FAITHFUL ANGELS

163

ANGELS ALL AROUND US

SEND ME AN ANGEL

When life seems dark and empty

and there's no hope in sight,

look for God to send an angel

to guide you toward the light.

❧❧❧

When the fearful heart longs for something to hold onto, when the despairing soul seeks strength to continue on, when the anxious mind reaches for comfort and hope . . . that is *When God Sends an Angel*.

It should come as no surprise that the original Hebrew translation of the word *angel* is *messenger*. Angels are God's chosen messengers of hope, love, and security in an ever-changing world. Their presence imparts evidence of something far grander than earthly illusions. Their words offer us clarity amidst the chaos of our times. And their love provides a glimpse of the indescribable nature of God.

What, exactly, is an angel? What does an angel look like, sound like, act like? Many of us have preconceived notions of what an angel may be, pieced together from biblical descriptions, fine art, and movies and television shows. Who among us is unfamiliar with the image of the mighty archangels, the glorious seraphim, the adorable and chubby cherubs? In our imaginations, we conjure impressive silken wings, soft flowing robes, and golden halos. We imagine ethereal creatures hovering in midair, surrounded by heavenly light as they dispense love, hope, and guidance to the frightened and the hopeless below.

But God sends angels in forms we may fail to recognize, and it's up to us to hear and act upon their messages. Angels can come in all shapes, sizes, and forms: as good friends who support our deepest dreams; as neighbors who go out of their way to help us; as pets that sense when we're in danger; as strangers who offer us a hand just when we need it most.

God sees everyone as a potential angel—even *you* can become someone's angel. You never know when you might be called upon, so pay attention to that urging, that feeling that tells you to call your mother, check on a friend, or even just say a kind word to a passing stranger. Who knows? Maybe the hungry man asking for food on the street corner has been sent by God with a very important message just for you. Perhaps the security guard working the night shift has been sent to protect you in a time of danger. Or, just maybe, the woman sitting near you on the bus, the one you've been "stuck" next to all day, is telling you something you need to hear.

There are many people throughout our lives who act as angels: They inspire, uplift, and encourage us. They also protect us and comfort us. Some angels come into our lives just when we need them—others are there for an extended time, and only gradually do we come to recognize them as angels. Some angels connect us to a loved one we have lost, to let us know that person is okay or to allow us to finally feel closure.

Sometimes we experience angelic intervention in the form of amazing coincidence and spectacular serendipity, only to pass it off as luck. Or we struggle with a difficult choice— only to pass off that still, small voice whispering in our ear as intellect. Or perhaps we have a powerful and insightful vision that leads to an answer we have been seeking, only to pass it off as a dream—but our souls know what our minds cannot discern. God has sent an angel.

None of us walk the earth alone; we all have access to our very own guardians who take us by the hand and lead us into the light of a better life. It's our job to recognize these angels when they present themselves. It's our job to hear their messages. In order to call upon the angels and receive the blessings they impart, we must learn to actively listen with an open and willing heart. If we choose not to hear their message, or if somehow it slips past our comprehension, how can we act upon it?

Let the stories in *When God Sends an Angel* teach you how to listen. Let these stories guide you toward the miracles that accompany the presence of angels. Let them be a beacon of hope leading you out of the darkness and into the light. Let these stories create within you a strong faith in the power of angels and their ability to make your life meaningful and joyful.

In the beautiful and inspiring collection of stories contained within *When God Sends an Angel,* you will meet angels who seem divine yet ordinary. You will read stories of hope restored, of love renewed, of life redeemed. Share the comfort and inspiration of others' encounters with angels, and believe, if you didn't believe already, that angels are present in everyone's lives—even yours.

GUIDING ANGELS

Angels find us, not only when we need them most, but even when we think we are fine on our own.

❧❧❧

STRANGER ON THE STREET

Oh, I felt good about myself. I was so pleased with what a nice, kind, thoughtful person I was. I'd just spent hours laboring away at volunteer tasks, giving my time to help others. I'd helped take care of patients in a nursing home, reading letters to them, chatting with them. My head was full of self-congratulation. I was feeling incredibly virtuous, wonderfully delighted with myself, absolutely superior to lesser folk who were too selfish and preoccupied to reach out to those in need.

Fully absorbed in myself, I scarcely noticed the grubby stranger heading my way. He aimed straight at me as if I was the only person out on the streets that day. When I suddenly noticed him, I braced myself. Uh-oh. I could see his filthy clothes, torn and stained. Clearly he'd spent months on the streets, perhaps living in doorways or beneath bridges, huddled in boxes or wrapped in newspapers for warmth.

I dreaded the confrontation. Being approached by homeless people made me feel immensely uncomfortable. If I gave someone cash, it might be used badly. Besides, I didn't have much money myself. Every penny counted. In fact, I was walking home to save bus fare. With the coins I'd saved, I could buy myself a little treat, maybe an ice-cream cone. I'd earned a treat. I deserved it.

As the stranger approached, I tensed. It was my money, after all. I worked hard to earn it. I had a right to keep what I'd earned. I had a right to spend it the way I wanted. I shouldn't be expected to give away my hard-earned cash! Braced and tense, I watched as he drew near.

"Can you spare a few cents?" he asked, his hand extended.

I drew back without actually moving. I thought of the money in my purse. So little of it. And it was mine, all mine.

I opened my mouth to make excuses, to tell him I didn't have any money, to lie and brush him away. His eyes pierced mine as I spoke, and I found myself telling him the truth, or at least part of it.

"I don't have much money. Nothing to spare," I told him. In a way, it was true. But those eyes pierced right through me.

"I understand," he told me, his voice deep and steady. And I thought he did understand. Exactly. I thought he saw right through me, into my greedy spirit. I thought he knew somehow just how much money I carried and what I planned to do with it. He seemed to see into my heart and hear the echo of my childish desires. It was my money. I didn't want to share. Why should I? I wanted it for myself.

Still holding my gaze, he said, "I have not always been as you see me now," and then he walked away, back straight, dignified in his ragged clothes. He passed behind me, and I stood, stricken and bereft, ashamed of myself.

How could I be so selfish, so unkind? Even with so little cash, I could share what I had. I could treat us both to some small treat. We could go together to a nearby snack bar. My money would surely stretch for us both.

I whirled to call him back, but he was gone. In those moments when I was feeling shame for having been selfish, he'd disappeared.

I never saw him again. But in that moment, staring down an empty sidewalk, I knew. That homeless stranger in his bedraggled clothing had known I wasn't as good and kind and thoughtful as I liked to think I was. He'd known the hidden selfishness in me. He'd known me.

And suddenly I knew him. He'd given me a clue, hadn't he? He'd told me that he hadn't always been as I saw him then. And I thought of the words in the Bible that urge hospitality to strangers because you never know when you might be entertaining an angel.

For that was what he was. I'm as sure of it as I am of anything. That homeless, ragged stranger, begging coins of me, had been sent to remind me that I was nowhere near as good as I thought I was.

I thought about those moments for a long time. I rehearsed what I should have told him, what I wished I'd said. I practiced conversations in case he returned to give me another chance. I searched for his face on my walks from then on. But he didn't return. I guess he'd done what he meant to do. He'd taught me a valuable lesson about myself and others. He'd taught me not to think so highly of myself, not to feel so pleased with me. And he taught me not to judge others too easily.

Behind the next stranger in rags there might lurk an angel in disguise.

Do not forget to entertain strangers, for by so doing some people have entertained angels without knowing it.

—HEBREWS 13:2

A Life-Changing Decision

"Excuse me, could you help me?" called an older woman I'd never seen before. One moment I'd been striding through the store aisle, intent on my errands, the next I found myself interrupted by a stranger.

My immediate thought was that she'd mistaken me for a salesperson. I was rushing to get my shopping done before my three children got out of school, so I assumed I could set this woman straight and then be on my way.

"Which of these bedspreads do you think would be best?" the woman asked, holding up the packaged items. I felt puzzled. Why ask me? She didn't know me. I didn't know her. Why would she want my opinion? Perhaps she wondered which spread cost more or which would wash well or which one would last the longest.

But, no. She held up the spreads for me to study and waited, anxiously, for me to offer my opinion.

"They're both nice," I told her, still feeling baffled. What did my opinion matter?

"Yes," she agreed, "but I can't decide which would look better in my bedroom."

I stared into her worried eyes, noting the creases on her brow. I felt even more confused. This wasn't a major, life-altering decision. She was only deciding on a bedspread. She could flip a coin, or she could return one if she got it home and changed her mind. Yet, her eyes seemed to tell me this was an important moment. I pushed away the irritability that had begun to rise in me and settled in to help her.

"What does your bedroom look like?" I asked.

We discussed the color of paint on the walls, the shade of the drapes, and the flecks of color in the carpet. We talked about putting throw pillows on the bed to bring out the blue in one of the spreads. We went over how the blue flowers would light up the plainer drapes and carpeting.

After long debate and consideration, we chose her new bedspread. She smiled, her face suddenly smooth of worry creases, her eyes alight with eagerness to get her new bedspread home and in place.

"Thank you so much for helping," she said earnestly, clasping the packaged bedspread to her chest. "I can't tell you how much it means."

"That's OK," I told her, still a little puzzled.

"I'm a widow," she revealed hesitantly. "My husband just recently died. Until then, we had made every decision together. It just hit me today, standing here alone, that he'll never be with me to make decisions again, and I felt so shaken and lonely. Thank you so much for being here. I'll be OK now."

Then she hurried away with her new bedspread, toward the life she was facing with renewed courage and determination. And suddenly I felt immensely thankful that I'd taken the time to help a stranger. I felt deeply glad and humbled that I'd been able to help in some small way, that my advice had eased the pain and pressure of her first independent choice. I vowed right then never to be too busy to help another person in need.

Angels awaken my mind to possibilities—
On earth,
In heaven,
And in myself.

ENJOYING THE BEAUTY

"*I*s anyone from out of state?" the tour guide asked, gazing around the bus and smiling at us.

I raised my hand.

"Where are you from?"

"Florida," I said. *Where there is nothing to compare with the beauty of autumn we're seeing here*, I felt like adding.

While we waited for our afternoon tour to begin, I asked the lady next to me where she lived.

"St. Charles," she said, adding, "You know, I was here last week, and the leaves were stupendous on that tour."

"They look lovely today," I said. "And it's a perfect day."

The temperature was around 74, the sun shone brightly, and a gentle breeze rustled the leaves. I felt like a tourist who had just discovered a gold mine. Although I had passed this arboretum every day on my way to junior college years before, I had taken it all for granted back then.

As the tour began, the lady next to me said, "I notice a lot of leaves have fallen since last week. That tour was just perfect."

"That's nice," I said and turned my attention to the tour guide, who told us about Mr. Morton, the owner of the

Morton Salt company, who decided to build an estate here, which eventually became the Morton Arboretum.

As we rode along, the tour guide pointed out different trees and clusters of trees. "Oohs" and "aahs" came out of my mouth each time I turned to where she pointed.

"Look over there," the lady next to me said. "See that cluster of bare trees? Those had gorgeous red leaves on them last week. It was breathtaking."

I looked at the bare trees and tried hard not to think about what I had missed.

What about the breathtaking view on our right? I almost asked.

"Yes, those leaves last week were so beautiful—this is nothing compared to last week," Ms. Party Pooper rambled on.

Well, it's something for me. I haven't seen autumn leaves in years, I argued in my mind. I looked around again to see another beautiful grove of trees.

Soon we were deep in the forest. My neighbor told me again and again how the beauty of these leaves wasn't nearly as wonderful as those she'd seen last week. Then suddenly we were surrounded by yellow; sugar maples stretched in every direction. The tour guide stopped the bus.

"Wow! This is great," I said, enraptured by the gorgeous colors surrounding us. My neighbor was silent, but only for a moment.

"This tour guide is not as good as last week's," she whispered, shaking her head.

In the midst of my anger at this woman for wrecking my nature adventure, a gentle whisper came to my soul: *You act like her sometimes.*

As I compared the beauty of these trees to the wonder of God's love, I saw how many times I acted like this lady, keeping my mind on what God had done in the past and comparing those miracles, vainly, to present negative events—the bare trees in my life. I thought about how when I became too focused on the pressures of life, I no longer sensed God's presence, his amazing love for me, and the beautiful things he had brought into my life.

At first I felt pretty bad about getting "stuck" next to that lady. I've since concluded that maybe she was in a "bare trees" phase of her life. Now when I think back to that day, I'm thankful for her. Through her, God showed me there will always be obstacles to sensing his love, the beauty of the world, and the beauty of people around me—obstacles that come both from within and from outside myself.

Today I choose to look beyond bare trees and see the beauty all around me.

Angels reflect the magnificence of heaven, the spectacular home that God has prepared for all those who belong to him.

No Exit

I waited for the answering service to connect the caller. Crisis-line volunteers never answer directly. Rarely do we talk to a client more than once or twice, so I was surprised when I recognized the voice on the other end of the line. It was Denise, a young woman I'd spoken to a couple of times in the past. Both times she'd been badly beaten by her husband, and both times I'd encouraged her to go to the women's shelter to avoid further abuse.

"I can't leave him," she'd said. "I have to stay."

When I heard her voice this time, I felt a mixture of relief and concern. At least she was not in a hospital or, worse yet, the morgue. She was probably calling after yet another beating.

I carried the phone to the kitchen and poured a cup of coffee as I listened.

"I'm so glad it's you," she said, when I introduced myself. "I really just called because I hoped they could get a message to you. I wanted to tell you about a strange thing that happened."

"Strange" was not how I'd have described her past beatings, and she wasn't whispering as abuse victims often do. Something must have happened.

Denise didn't wait for my response. "Remember I told you that our office was moving downtown, and that Dan wanted me to quit when he heard. He was so jealous because I'd be meeting new people.

"Well," she went on, "last Friday I agreed to work late to get the new office set up. Everyone else had already left when I finished. I hurried to collect my things and head home. I knew if I was too late, Dan would accuse me of playing around with another man."

Why, I wondered, did abusive spouses always seem obsessed with the idea that their partners were cheating?

"Anyway," Denise continued, "when I went downstairs to go through the main entrance, it was locked...chained shut from the inside. I wasn't worried at first. After all, a big office building like that had to have lots of exits."

While Denise talked, I recorded her information on the crisis call form.

"I checked the door at the end of the nearest hall," she said. "There was a sign that said 'No Exit.' I tried it anyway, but it wouldn't open. I checked several other doors. Each had a 'No Exit' sign. By then I was getting panicked. I could just imagine the punishment Dan would have in store for me for being so late."

I could imagine it too...and the longer it took for her to get home, the worse the beating would probably be.

Denise went on. "I was nearly frantic by then, running furiously back and forth. I spotted a fire escape and rushed to it. Once more I was met by a 'No Exit' sign. The fine print explained that in case of fire, all the fire doors would automatically open."

Poor Denise. I understood her fear and frustration.

"By then," she said, "I was terrified. I ran back to the front door and began banging on it. 'Get me out of here,' I yelled. I thought maybe somebody outside would hear me, though I don't know what I thought they'd do. Then I realized someone was behind me. I quickly turned around. An older man was standing there. I was sobbing by then," Denise told me, "and I explained that there was no way out."

" 'There's always a way out,' he said reassuringly. 'Follow me.'

"I followed him through the dark hall to a door I'd not noticed before. It was locked just like the others, but my rescuer reached into the pocket of his jacket and pulled out a key. He unlocked the door. I thanked him and hurried to my car. I still hated to think what would happen when I got home. I got my cell phone out of the glove compartment to call Dan, but even as I dialed our number I thought of the man's words: 'There's always a way out.' I remembered you'd said that, too, when you gave me the number for the women's shelter. I still had the number in my purse. Instead of calling Dan, I called the shelter. That's where I am now."

I breathed a sigh of relief. She was safe!

"Thank heaven for the security guard," I said. "I'm so glad you listened to him. Now you know that there is always a way out."

"I just had to follow the signs," Denise agreed. "Thank heaven."

How many angels are there?
One—who transforms our life—is plenty.

—TRADITIONAL SAYING

THE AIRPLANE

I was walking to work like I do every late afternoon, carrying the same small, battered brown paper shopping bag I always do. I happened to be heading up Fifth Avenue that afternoon, and I got one of those looks I sometimes get from someone smartly dressed and successful. It makes me feel small, like a man who hasn't made much of himself in life. I hold down a part-time evening job in a midtown firm, so at work nobody cares how I dress. My shoes are badly worn, and my pants have been washed a few too many times, as have my shirts.

That splendid autumn day, when the traffic light changed to red, I was stopped in the close cluster of people gathered at the curb.

"I need help crossing the street," someone was repeating. "Could someone help me across the street?" I turned and looked. It was a blind man. He was dumpy, messy, and disgusting-looking. Squat and chubby, he looked more like a boy grown old than a man.

The light changed. Figuring someone else would tend to the guy, I hurried on. Behind me, I could hear him repeating the same plea over and over. I was almost across the street when some note in his voice caused me to stop in my tracks and turn around. I watched person after person do exactly as I had done. The blind man stood pathetically in the same spot, repeating the same words. A pretty blond in a business suit whisked by him to get out of the way. Another attractive young office worker did the same. Something in the scene nailed me to the spot. I was mesmerized by the futility I heard in the man's voice. The light changed. I had to get out of the street.

I dashed back across to where the man was standing, alone and lost. "I'll help you," I announced. Even as I said this I regretted it. What possessed me to say it? I was running late for work, and his problems weren't my concern. Well, it was too late now to take back my offer. I stood there with him, a little off to one side, waiting for the light to change again. It was uncomfortable.

"I need help crossing the street," the man repeated, not sure if I was still there.

"I'm right here," I assured him. "I'm going to help you across."

He reached out then and put his hand on my coat sleeve. I couldn't help recoiling in aversion. The light changed. I led him across the street.

"There," I announced when we reached the far curb.

"I need to go to 38th Street," he now informed me, "and then I have to turn and go one block west."

"I'm on my way to work," I protested.

He was silent, helpless.

"I can take you as far as 38th Street," I relented and began walking again.

"You don't know how to walk with a blind person, do you?" he blurted after a few steps. I looked at his face, into his vacant eyes. What did this man want from me? He was making me anxious. The way he was dressed was sloppy and unkempt, and his overcoat was stained. He wasn't the kind of person I wanted to be close to.

"How are you supposed to walk with a blind person?" I sniped in frustration, at the end of my rope with this guy. I was walking with him, wasn't I?

He slid his hand around my elbow and grabbed the crook of my arm.

I immediately stiffened. Tense and irritated, I let him hold onto my arm as we walked. I didn't speak, nor did he. We walked for almost a block without uttering a word. All of a sudden, though, I realized the two of us had been talking all along—through our body language. He could tell, I was convinced, from my stiff arm and attempt at distancing myself, that he repulsed me. He probably felt hurt, made small, by a message I hadn't even been aware I was sending him. At that moment, I saw him not as undesirable but as deprived. Without thinking, I started to speak.

"It's a splendid fall day, and there's a good mood on the street," I began, looking around and describing whatever presented itself. "All around us people are coming and going. They're all very well dressed and look happy. It seems like they're shopping. They're going in and out of the stores, carrying shopping bags loaded with the things they've bought.

"The store windows all along the street are decorated and pretty," I continued. "We're walking by a store now that sells men's clothes. Across the street there's a big store that sells nothing but computers. Down the way is Lord & Taylor, with a row of American flags flying out in front. The traffic is heavy today—lots of cars and trucks. Even though traffic isn't moving very quickly, it's a bit odd that no one is honking or seems to be in a great hurry."

He was silent, giving no indication that he'd even heard me. I continued, "The sun is getting low in the sky and beginning to reflect off the tall buildings up by 42nd Street. The windows look like they're on fire. There's not a single cloud in the sky. It's a perfect, pure blue sky."

Still, the man didn't speak. "And," I added, almost as an afterthought, "way, way up high there's a single airplane going overhead. It's up so high, you can't even hear its noise. Now the sun's reflection is flashing off it."

I fell silent. The two of us walked along as before.

All of a sudden, the man spoke.

"There's an airplane up there?" he inquired with the eager voice of a five-year-old.

"Well, it's not in sight anymore," I qualified. "It flew by. There's just a slice of blue sky we can see, because of the tall buildings on each side of the street. It disappeared behind the buildings."

"What kind of plane was it?" he pressed me. "Did you see what kind of plane it was?"

I was at a loss. I didn't know the first thing about airplanes. "It was some kind of passenger plane," I hazarded vaguely, "the kind that airlines use."

"How big was it?" he pleaded, as if the plane itself held up the whole sky and put it in place above his head for the first time so that he walked now in a world made much bigger than before.

No matter how inept my fumbling answers, he shot out one question after another about that tiny speck of a plane in the sky that I'd only glimpsed for a fleeting second. He couldn't stop inquiring about it—until we were standing on the corner of 38th Street. I stopped and stood there with him at the curb as people rushed by in various directions. "This is where you turn off," I announced.

I shook his hand. "It's been a real pleasure walking with you," I told him sincerely. I was sure he knew I meant it. He could feel it in my hand and in my voice. And then I singled out a stunning young lady about to cross the street. "Excuse me," I addressed her, "this man needs help getting where he's going. It's only one block west."

Maybe because I didn't see him as disgusting anymore, she didn't either. "I'm going that way," she said gladly.

"Here's a beautiful woman," I said to him, "who's going to take you where you're going." I put his hand on her arm and gave it a quick pat.

I stood on the busy sidewalk a moment before proceeding on to work, watching the two of them disappear into the crowd crossing the street.

We are most like angels when
we stand ready to serve
the good inside of us.

NEW PLACES, NEW TRADITIONS

"Life's a trade-off," Nancy reminded herself as she navigated her car through unfamiliar streets. A bad job for a good job. Small apartment for half a house. But Georgia sunshine for Massachusetts snow? Nancy shook her head at her folly, peering into the swirling snow for street signs. Her three children sat quietly behind her, too exhausted to squabble or pick at each other.

"The good news is that we have a place to live," Nancy said, trying to sound cheerful in the spirit of the season. The little town looked like a Christmas card, except for one dark house among a block of cheery-looking homes. Nancy's heart sank as she turned into the driveway of the dark house. The porch light came on, and an older woman peered over the porch railing as they emerged from the car.

The kids swallowed hard and shrank back against the upholstered seat backs.

"This isn't our house, is it Mommy?" Kaitlin inquired, her voice diminishing almost to a whisper as she realized that yes, this was the house.

"You're late," the woman noted sternly.

"We got stuck in a snowdrift," Nancy replied.

"It takes hearty souls to live here. Come along then." With that, the woman turned abruptly and led them into the first floor of the house. Recently widowed, Josephine was reluctantly taking in boarders, as she preferred to call them. In reality, her family home had been divided into two spacious apartments. The house's loveliness caught Nancy by surprise: pristine hardwood floors and woodwork, tall ceilings, and the aroma of lemon polish that had kept built-in cupboards and bookcases gleaming for more than a hundred years. The parlor had been converted into two bedrooms, the living room into another bedroom and den. The kitchen, with glass-front cupboards, held a small round oak table and four chairs.

"My family and I always sat there," said Josephine. She turned away and then paused at the foot of the back staircase. "The doctors and my busybody children say I have to leave my door unlocked in case I have another spell. I don't plan to. I'll not bother you, and I expect the same. Good night."

The family slowly began to settle in. Nancy registered the kids at their new school, and she was welcomed with open arms at the teaching hospital where she'd been hired. At home, however, a frigid chill remained. Josephine avoided contact with her tenants except when there was something to criticize, such as sleds parked too close to the driveway or noisy snowball fights. The children began to hide when they saw her coming. Nancy invited her for coffee, but Josephine turned her down.

Among the last boxes Nancy and the children unpacked were the Christmas decorations. Homesickness quickly descended like a fog.

"New places, new traditions," Nancy said to her children, reaching for a wreath. After decorating, they gathered around the old oak table, laughing, reminiscing, and dreaming. Overhead in her apartment, Josephine walked back and forth in sharp paces, disapprovingly it seemed. Seen from the street, the darkness upstairs contrasted sharply with the shining main floor, which was now gaily lit with candles at the windows, handmade decorations, and a towering tree. Well, thought Nancy, there are no magnolia leaves, pepperberries, or fresh holly, but the lonely heart accepts what it is offered.

She was leaving for work one day soon after when she heard Josephine on the porch talking to the postal carrier. The mail carrier sounded jovial as he mentioned the festivities he was looking forward to this season.

"No, it certainly isn't a merry Christmas," Josephine muttered, "and I'm most definitely not going to decorate this year. There's not much to celebrate, if you ask me."

The poor carrier fled as Nancy leaned out of sight against the door. She recognized loneliness when she met it, for it was lodged in her own heart, too.

"Get in the car," Nancy called to her children from the car that afternoon, pulling up beside them as they walked home from school, chatting and laughing with each other. "We've got Christmas mischief to make."

As soon as Josephine left for choir practice that evening, Nancy and the children raced upstairs with a small tree and ornaments they had bought. Taking a deep breath, they entered the forbidden but unlocked connecting door into Josephine's apartment. In record time, they set up the tiny tree and decorated it with homemade paper chains and ornaments borrowed from their own tree. When Nancy flipped on the switch, the tree's colored lights twinkled bravely against the darkened windows.

They were eating supper in their own apartment when Josephine returned. They held their breath as she trudged upstairs. Nothing happened. Nancy's heart sank.

"At least the tree didn't come flying out a window," she told her children, managing a smile.

But the next morning, they discovered an invitation slipped underneath the back door.

"Supper tonight. Josephine." And a poignant postscript, "Please come."

The house smelled of baking bread when Nancy and the children climbed the stairs that evening. After they enjoyed vegetable soup and homemade French bread, Josephine, at the children's insistence, carried out the old manger scene she had mentioned during dinner. There were also some hand-carved reindeer that needed to come out of the attic.

Before Josephine knew it, she was immersed in celebration of the season.

Soup supper became one of many traditions that Nancy, the children, and Josephine shared. For as each of them adapted to their new situations, they learned creative ways to remember the past, be grateful for the present, and look forward to the future. Throughout the years they celebrated holidays, birthdays, and various other milestones together. But mostly they celebrated family and friendship—the cornerstones of any good tradition.

If you've looked to the stars at night
to find an angel chorus, you've done well.
If you've looked into your heart
to find the angel's song, you've done better.

GOD IS SO WONDERFUL

*C*hristmas was always a hard time of year for me, and this particular Christmas Eve, about 40 years ago, was no different. I was 19 years old and about halfway through beauty school. My schedule was hectic, and, I'm ashamed to say, when the supervisor told me about my next customer I got especially irritated. The lady coming in was in a wheel-chair and almost completely disabled. I knew this customer would take extra time, and I was already feeling swamped.

Once the woman's hair was washed and her caregiver left, we had a chance to talk. She was probably in her fifties at the time, and she told me that the previous year she had lost her husband and her only child, a son. The only family members she had left were a couple of cousins.

She hesitated a moment and, with a beautiful smile on her face, said, "But you know, God is so wonderful that he gave me naturally curly hair so I wouldn't have to worry about taking care of it. What a blessing!"

Talk about putting life into perspective.

I still think of that woman almost every day. No matter what circumstances I face, I still hear her smiling voice saying, "God is so wonderful." She never knew what an impact that simple statement had on me, but I thank God for sending her into my life just when I needed her most.

THE EYE OF THE BEHOLDER

Shoving the vacuum into its stall in the hall closet, I stifled a groan. A half-day of housework behind me and I still wasn't ready for the out-of-state company expected any minute. My four small cyclones whirled past, leaving a wake of toys, crumbs, and stray shoes scattered across the recently trackless carpet.

And then I saw them: the sliding doors of the family room that opened onto the patio. The very doors I had washed and scrubbed earlier that morning now boasted generous finger streaks and tiny nose prints all over the freshly polished glass panes.

"And that looks like . . . ." Frowning, I stepped nearer and bent for a closer inspection. "It is! Peanut butter! Those kids! It's impossible to get this house clean."

Near tears, I plopped onto the couch and grabbed the jangling phone.

"Hello?" I sighed in exasperation.

"Hello, dear," I heard my mother's voice, a state away. "Are you busy?"

"Oh, you have no idea! We're expecting guests, and I just can't seem to get all the housework caught up around here, and the kids . . . "

"That reminds me," she interrupted. "I should do some of my own. Housework, that is."

"You? Huh! You have no idea what a dirty house even looks like," I whined. "After all, there's only the two of you. What can there possibly be to clean?"

"Welllll...," she drawled, with a smile in her voice, "the mirror above the couch is smeared. But you know, dear, every time I look at the sweet baby prints your little ones left there last month, I can't bring myself to wipe them away. I'm still showing off those precious kisses and streaks as priceless artwork to my friends!"

I caught my breath at the perfect timing of the messenger and her message. Oh, Mother understood—with both her remembering heart and her heaven-sent perspective. With her dual status as mother and grandmother, she could look back and beyond.

I gazed around the room. A half-eaten cracker here, over there some wadded-up socks, tilting towers of books in the corner. And four tracks of tiny footprints framing it all.

And crowning it all was a hand-painted masterpiece on the patio doors. Unnumbered. One of a kind. I grinned.

My own piece of priceless artwork.

Angels bring a heavenly dimension to everyday life.

LESSONS FROM LUCY

Sometimes big lessons come to us in small packages. That was certainly the case when my husband and I adopted a kitten from a local animal shelter. We thought a kitten would make a fun addition to the family. We didn't realize how much time and attention she would need—or what a treasure she would be.

Like small children, kittens require three basic things: a lot of love, a lot of attention, and a lot of patience. They also need constant monitoring to keep them out of dangerous situations. Our kitten—who we named "Lucy" because of her Lucille Ball–like "Waaaaaaa!"—came home from the shelter the same day her little eight-week-old body had been spayed. The veterinarian and the shelter employees assured me she would be fine if she was kept quiet and still. With her scar still fresh, and a respiratory problem to boot (common for animals acquired at shelters), Lucy required total attention for the first few days. And I mean total, from morning until bedtime.

Lucy apparently had no idea she had just had surgery, or that she had a cold. All she knew was that she was in her new home, and she wanted to explore! I, in turn, had to follow her everywhere to keep her out of trouble. This was not easy for someone like me, who always has deadlines to meet and countless tasks to complete as a writer, business owner, and ministerial student. My life was so busy and full of career demands and goals, I was accustomed to a hectic pace in my day-to-day existence. But suddenly, I was forced to stop the frantic freight train I had been riding and get used to a slower speed of life. I spent hours at a time just watching that tiny, wheezing little creature run all over the house. Exhausted, she would eventually crawl up on my chest and go to sleep. And once she positioned herself comfortably, she wasn't about to move.

As Lucy's health improved, she proved herself to be a four-legged dervish, not at all the sweet, quiet kitty we had seen in the cage at the animal shelter. The peace I had hoped for once she got well enough to play on her own seemed increasingly out of reach. She wanted to play, all right, but she wanted to play with me. And how could I possibly resist that sweet, furry face, that whiny little "Waaaaaaa"? She would run back and forth, chase shoelaces, and generally be a little terror. But then she'd climb onto my chest with her crooked four-legged gait, put her face up against my cheek, and snooze two or three hours away as though she had all the time in the world. During these sleeping spells, her breathing would be full and clear, and I was hesitant to get up for fear she'd begin wheezing again. Sometimes I even dozed off myself—unheard of, for me!

In those quiet times, I was forced to stop thinking of my goals (and myself) and focus entirely on another living thing. I began to learn the joy of just doing nothing, of just being. Like Lucy, I began to sense that there was plenty of time to get things done and that these gentle hours were just as vital to a healthy, happy life as achievement and career fulfillment. I began looking forward to those hours, when I could just lie there and stare at Lucy's beautiful little tiger-striped face, stroking her soft fur as I wondered in amazement at God's ability to create such a perfect, adorable ball of fur and personality, and marveling at my luck in finding her.

Lucy taught me how to be patient, not just with a crazy, silly, lovable kitten, but with my life, my time, my goals, and my dreams. The feeling that there was more than enough time became a comfort and actually gave me more motivation and confidence than my previously panicked focus on deadlines and my "do-or-die" mentality. When we finally get quiet and still long enough, it's amazing how clearly and distinctly God's voice within us becomes. And God was clearly telling me to slow down and smell the roses, or, in this case, pet the kitten.

It seemed as if I couldn't get anything done the week Lucy arrived. But somehow, mysteriously, things got done anyway. I met all my deadlines, I made all my calls and sent all my faxes, and I answered all my e-mails. I even found myself with plenty of time left over to read, study, spend time with my family, watch a little baseball on TV, and start researching a few new articles that had been percolating in the back of my mind. It was as if I had learned not how to squeeze more time out of each day, but how to make better use of the time I had. Wow!

But none of those things seemed quite so important once I felt that soft little chin against my neck, nuzzling me and biting at my hair (and, sometimes, my ear!). That was enough to make me drop everything I was doing and just relish the sensation and the moment. I realized that there really is magic in the slow moments of life.

I learned all this from a tiny little temptress named Lucy, who needed nothing more in life than a shoestring and a soft body to sleep on to be happy. It seems teachers come in many shapes and sizes—and species!

Angels do the work of love—love around us, love within us, love compelling us, and love igniting us.

GET OUT OF THE ROUGH

*M*att warmed up with a few practice swings. It would be fun to play a round with his old high school teammates—even though the occasion wasn't a happy one. It was appropriate though, Matt thought as he pulled on his golfing glove. Coach Hunter would have loved the idea of his old golfers getting together for a game after his memorial service. And the sun's shining, it's a beautiful day, and I'm here with my old buddies, Matt thought with satisfaction, twisting the bill of his cap around to the back.

Matt wished his old coach was there with them so he could tell him about his new job. He was making more money than he'd ever dreamed possible. Who'd have thought he'd be making nearly a hundred grand just one year out of college? Matt's buddies were mighty impressed when he told them in response to their questions.

"I thought only gangsters pulled in that kind of dough," teased Brian.

"Or pro golfers," called Andy. "And you'll never be a professional."

Matt laughed.

When it was his turn to tee off, he had a clean hit down the middle of the fairway. A little short, but a good drive.

"Coach Hunter would have called us wimps if he'd caught us riding in this cart," said Brian as they bounced along the path toward their balls.

"He was a great man," said Matt. "He taught us as much about life as he taught us about golf." The men were silent for a few moments, thinking of the impact their mentor had on their lives.

To change the subject, Brian said, "So tell me about this high-paying dream job of yours. Are you a company big-wig, or what?"

"There are lots of good things about the job besides the money," said Matt.

He went on to explain that selling computer software to health and fitness centers was perfect for him because it combined his lifelong passion for sports with his interest in computers and technology. "But," he said as he pulled up to the next tee, "there are some aspects about the job I don't much like."

Matt and Brian didn't have a chance to get back to their conversation until the long fifth hole. "So what is it about the job you don't like?" asked Brian.

Matt frowned. "I don't think my company's any worse than most others, but it is sometimes hard to feel good about promising that software will arrive on a specific date and then not have it be there on time."

"That's probably the nature of the business," said Brian. He drove the cart into shade while they waited for the group ahead of them to putt in.

"It bothers me, too," said Matt, "that my bosses want me to tell customers that our new products will be compatible with their old computers. They may work, but they don't always work together very well."

Brian looked down the fairway. "Looks like the green is clear. You're away. Go for it."

Matt climbed out of the cart. He reached into his bag, pulled out his three iron, and walked over to his ball. Remembering to keep his head down and his hands firm, he got off a long, long drive.

He and Brian shielded their eyes to follow its flight path right toward the rough. It bounced once and then settled in the tall grass a short distance from the fairway. "I must have forgotten to focus on the direction I wanted the ball to travel."

"Guess we're all a little rusty," said Brian. "If you think you can find it, Andy and Kevin and I will hit."

"I'm pretty sure it's in the tall grass just beyond that second lodgepole pine. I'll flag you guys down if I don't find it pretty quickly."

As Matt walked along the edge of the fairway, he thought of another aspect of his job that bothered him. Just a couple of days earlier he'd learned how hard it was for his customers to cash in on the rebate he'd promised them. He'd rationalized that hardly any customers bothered to cash in on rebates anyway, but his discovery still made him uncomfortable.

The white object Matt had been walking toward turned out to be a duck feather rather than his ball. Changing direction, he carefully searched the ground in front of the large pine tree. Not spotting the ball, he looked all around the tree. There it was! His ball was sitting just on the edge of the rough but touching an out-of-bounds line.

Matt remembered a time five years earlier when he'd been in a similar spot. It was at the end of a long day of practice, and Matt was pushing toward his best score of the year. "Don't forget to count that as a penalty stroke," Coach Hunter had called out to him. Matt could hear his words as clearly now as if his old coach was standing beside him. "If you're not in bounds, you're out of bounds." Matt remembered . . . and understood the message. He realized why he'd received it. If you're not honest, you're dishonest . . . in life just as in golf.

Straddling the ball, he swung. The ball lofted out onto the fairway, not far from where his friends' balls rested. Matt stashed his club in his golf bag and hurried to where the other golfers were waiting.

"Your ball must have landed in a lucky spot," said Andy, impressed.

"You're right about that," said Matt. "I'll need to take a penalty stroke for being out of bounds, but I'm going to follow Coach Hunter's advice."

He got out his nine iron and chipped up onto the green. As soon as I get back home, he promised himself, I'm going to look for a job where I can stay in bounds all the time.

When I think of an angel, I think of a floating,
celestial being. I think of an angel
as someone who has only good thoughts, never bad.
I see them always with an eternal glow
and always pleasant and completely centered.
I picture them with such a sense of purpose,
so connected to their reason for being,
that they never lose their way.
I see angels as the kind of being I would like to be.

LOVING ANGELS

When you live with a heart of compassion, you have the heart of an angel. When you fill your life with deeds of compassion, you do the work of an angel.

❦

FROM THE HEART OF A CHILD

The storms that hit the counties east of us were the most devastating we had ever known in the state of Oklahoma. While our own neighborhood was spared, we had to watch as towns just miles away were flattened. I tried to spare my eight-year-old daughter, Amy, from the horror, but she heard about it from her schoolmates and insisted on watching the local evening news.

Amy watched, transfixed, as the reporters showed the extensive damage and the stunned, frightened families that no longer had homes to call their own. One reporter focused on the family of a young boy named Danny. The boy was devastated at the loss of his new puppy, Albert. The little beagle had panicked and escaped from the cellar where the family was hiding when a twister smashed through their house. The strong winds threw Albert against a wall, and rescue workers recovered his body there.

Amy sat silently, lost in thought, after seeing that report. When she finally stood up, she ran into her room and closed the door. We followed her a moment later, intending to console her, but when we opened her bedroom door, she wasn't crying. She was counting money on her bedspread. Her ceramic angel bank lay in pieces beside her, and Amy looked up with huge, hopeful eyes and told us her plan.

She intended to use her $4.12 to buy a new puppy for Danny. I immediately tried to talk her out of it, informing her that the boy had no home to keep the dog in, and that the price of a new beagle was way more than what she could afford. Purebred pups went for several hundred dollars. But Amy wouldn't hear of my adult excuses. She just shook her head and said that there were plenty of nice puppies at the local pound and that surely there would be a beagle there.

My husband looked at me with one of those what-do-we-do-now looks, and I shrugged, hoping that as the days passed Amy would forget Danny and Albert and beagle puppies. But three days later, Amy was tugging at my blouse, asking if today was the day we would go and pick out the puppy. I barely got out a protest when the phone rang. I answered it, and was surprised to find myself talking to the news reporter who had told Danny's story on TV!

Apparently, Amy had called the news station herself and asked for the reporter, who had been out on a story at the time. Now, the woman, Linda Hayes, was telling me all about Danny's family and what shelter they were staying at and how wonderful she thought my daughter was to use her own money to make a little boy happy.

What could I say, except that, yes, my daughter really was pretty wonderful. I arranged a time to meet Linda and her camera crew at the local animal shelter. When we arrived, Amy raced off to look for the perfect puppy. I shouted after her, but she was nowhere to be found until Linda's camera operator spotted her playing with a tiny puppy in a cage.

"Mama, look! He's perfect!" Amy squealed. She squealed with delight when a shelter employee let Rudy out of his cage to meet us. The puppy ran to Amy and begged to be picked up. As Amy held him close, I had a funny feeling that I would be buying not one, but two puppies that day.

As we paid for Rudy, Linda interviewed Amy. I had whispered to Linda that I wanted to surprise my daughter with a puppy of her own and that it might be fun to reveal our secret on camera. But Amy never gave her a chance. She was intent on delivering Rudy to Danny. Linda looked at me, and I nodded that we would go to Plan B.

We headed to Red Rock Elementary School, the temporary shelter where Danny's family was staying. Linda found the family, and we quietly talked with the parents about Amy's intentions, hoping they would be open to the idea despite the tremendous loss they had suffered. Not only were they open to it, they were moved to tears, amazed that a little girl had cared enough to do this for their child.

Danny sat quietly nearby, but the minute Amy walked up to him with Rudy in her arms the light went on in his gray-blue eyes. He stared at the dog, as if in shock. Amy handed the pup over and whispered, "He's yours. His name is Rudy, but you can call him Albert if you want to." There was not a dry eye in the school as Danny and Rudy were introduced, and an instant bond was formed.

It was a scene my family would view again later that evening on the local news. Watching Amy smile at Danny playing with his new puppy made my heart swell. I could barely keep from bursting into tears.

My husband went outside and called for Amy to come out. When I got up to follow and saw the look on Amy's face as she was presented with a yapping little beagle pup of her own, my tears let loose like a waterfall. I was so filled with joy and pride and gratitude as I watched a very special little girl fall in love with a puppy of her own.

Does everyone have an angel?
I'd like to believe it's true.
But if ever there's a shortage,
I'd gladly share mine with you.

THE MEANING OF CHARITY

T'ed Turner donated one billion dollars to the United Nations. Bill Gates and his wife have given billions more to worthy causes through their charitable foundation. But when I think about the true meaning of charity, I think about my Uncle Louie.

Lou Ruderman was not a rich man. He was just a regular working-class guy. He didn't have billions of dollars, but he gave in such a way that he helped keep a family of strangers alive. He did this twice a week for more than 20 years. And he never told a soul about it—not even his wife.

In the 1920s Lou Ruderman ran a grocery store in Carteret, New Jersey. But he lost it to the Depression in 1934. So he moved his wife and three young sons across the state to Trenton, where his brother-in-law helped him find work as a "meat jobber." Six days a week he rose before dawn and drove a refrigerated truck across the Delaware River into the packing house section of Philadelphia. He'd load up the truck with meat, then drive back and deliver the raw goods to small, independent grocery stores in the outlying areas of New Jersey.

He labored faithfully for his employer for ten years. Finally, with the encouragement and support of his wife, Goldie, an elementary school teacher, he scraped together enough money to buy a used truck and some supplies and strike out on his own.

Six days a week he drove his red truck labeled Louis Ruderman, Provisions and Meat Jobber. On days off from school, his sons accompanied him, singing Russian songs and nibbling cold hot dogs as they brought fresh meat to the mom-and-pop stores that dotted the Jersey landscape.

The stores served blacks, poor whites, and enclaves of Eastern European immigrants with whom Louie would joke and converse in Russian, Hungarian, Polish, and Yiddish. His relationships with the grocery store owners were close and personal, some lasting as long as 30 years.

He loved to laugh, play cards, and spend Sundays with his children and, eventually, his grandchildren. He never made much money, but somehow Louie managed to help all three of his sons attend medical school and become doctors.

One Sunday morning in 1968, he bought some bagels and fruit and went to visit his eldest son, Armand. His son opened the door, they exchanged greetings, and then Lou Ruderman pitched forward, the victim of a massive heart attack. He died in his son's arms. He was 71 years old.

A week later, an older African American woman showed up at my Aunt Goldie's door. The woman asked if this was the house where Lou Ruderman had lived. Goldie said it was. The woman nodded and said she had come to pay her respects.

My aunt was mystified. She'd never met this woman or heard anything about her. She thanked her for her kind words, then sheepishly said, "I'm sorry, but I don't know who you are." In the next few minutes Goldie discovered that after all these years, her husband still had a few secrets.

The woman explained that for more than 20 years, Lou Ruderman had been giving her family the leftover meat from his truck. Twice a week, 52 weeks a year, for over two decades, Lou Ruderman would show up in his little red truck and make sure her family didn't go hungry. Even though he'd been up since well before dawn, put in a full day's work hefting sides of beef and driving a truck, and had a wife and kids he ached to return to, he'd stop by and give the woman and her family whatever he could. He did it when the icy winds of February turned his fingers red. He did it when the suffocating humidity of August glued the sweat-drenched back of his shirt to the seat of his truck.

For 20 years, Louis Ruderman, meat jobber, had kept another family alive. He told no one about it—not even his wife. It was a private act of charity, something between him and his God.

In some respects, the privacy of his generosity was Louie's greatest gift to the family. The meat gave them sustenance, but the privacy gave them dignity. Perhaps losing the grocery store to the Depression helped Louie understand that even when people do their best, they may still need a little extra help.

Back on my aunt's porch, the silver-haired woman expressed her gratitude and stuffed a ten-dollar bill into Goldie's hand—not for the meat, but to pay back some money Louie had loaned her during a past financial bind. Goldie, with tears in her eyes, didn't know what to say. The woman left before she could even find out her name.

When Goldie told her grown sons about the woman and her story, they weren't surprised. As children riding along with their father, they'd seen him give food to needy strangers lots of times.

When I think of the meaning of charity, I think of my Uncle Louie. Very few of us can be like Ted Turner or Bill Gates, donating billions to fight hunger, disease, and poverty. But almost all of us can be like Uncle Louie. He didn't have a lot to give from his bank account, so he gave from his little red truck. And he gave from his heart.

Have you wished you could be an angel?
You can easily do it: Don't doubt it.
Just help someone in need, or do a good deed,
And never tell a soul about it.

Do You Deliver?

*I*mpatiently I shifted into reverse. I hated missing preschool so early in the year. My students were just getting used to having their moms leave, and now I was leaving them, too. I could have sent flowers, but I figured somebody should show up for Margaret's funeral.

Margaret had been my neighbor. She had died three days earlier, just short of her fortieth birthday. I only knew her age because I had read it in the paper. We hadn't really been close friends. None of the neighbors knew Margaret well, but I hoped that one or two of them would come to the funeral.

I stopped at the railroad crossing. The signal lights flashed, and the engine emitted its warning moan. I would probably be late. At least I didn't have to look for the church since both our families went to St. John's. Margaret belonged to the Rosary Society. Maybe some of the Society members would attend the service. Actually, there were only about five or six ladies in the group. As far as I knew, they didn't do much . . . just prayed mostly, and visited people in the hospital to hand out prayer cards.

I'd often encouraged Margaret to get more involved at church. "I bet you'd like being on Parish Council," I'd suggested. "Or how about teaching religious education classes?"

The train sped past. Margaret's life had sped past, too, before she'd even had a chance to accomplish much. She hadn't worked. She could have been active in PTA—they always needed officers. Or she could have served on the hospital board, instead of just praying for the patients.

Surely one or two of the nurses who'd cared for Margaret would come to the funeral. And her Scottish friends might be there, too. I'd always tried to get Margaret involved in planning the big festival they had each fall, but she'd never done much more than get together with some of the older women who'd been born in Scotland. They would probably show up.

The long, striped arms lifted, and the line of cars started across the track. I hoped I wouldn't be late. The church would be so sparsely filled that it wouldn't be easy to sneak in unnoticed. Unnoticed . . . that was Margaret. Even though she walked everywhere, briskly bent forward as if braced against the wind, she was as much a part of the scenery as the newspaper carrier or the neighborhood cats.

She'd been such a private person, she would never have even told me about her heart condition if I hadn't dragged it out of her. "The doctors said the walking saved me," she'd explained. That was before she'd gotten pregnant. She shouldn't have. They'd warned her, but she wanted a baby so badly, she'd gambled . . . and lost. The little girl she'd prayed for had not lived either. They were going to be buried together.

The sound of sirens broke the silence of the sunny September morning. In a panic, I glanced at my speedometer. I wasn't speeding, thank goodness, but I pulled over anyway to let the cars pass. State patrol cars, about 20 of them, swooped past me into the church parking lot. I breathed a sigh of relief when I realized they were coming to the funeral, not pursuing me. Margaret's husband, Pat, was a Colorado patrol officer, and his colleagues had arrived en masse.

It was nice that they'd come, I thought. With a group of people that size, the church certainly wouldn't seem so empty. I steered my car into the parking lot. It wasn't easy to find a space. There was also a bit of a backup at the front door. I realized why, when I finally made it into the church. It was full!

Father was asking people to move toward the middle to make room for everyone. The service was just starting. I squeezed in and stared around in disbelief. From the looks of all the flowers on the altar, more people knew Margaret than I'd realized.

The fragrance of flowers mingled with the smell of the incense that the deacon was swinging over the casket. Father began the opening prayers. I pulled my card for Pat from my purse. I didn't want to forget to put it on the table after the service. In my note I'd written about how Margaret had taken over the laundry when our baby had been in Children's Hospital. I only knew that Margaret had been there because there was a prayer card on the table. I wanted Pat to know that she'd left comfort along with the clean clothes.

Father McGuire's words pushed through my thoughts. "Today," he said, "before the homily, there are some folks who would like to tell about how Margaret touched their lives." A young man limped slightly as he made his way up the aisle and stood behind the lectern. He told us that he had been in a horrible accident and had a leg amputated as a result. He pulled up one pant leg to show his prosthesis. He'd been considering suicide, he said, when a strange lady with a Scottish accent had appeared beside him. She'd talked and prayed him through the crisis.

Next, an older lady slowly took her place at the microphone. When her husband died, she explained, Margaret had stayed with her until her grandson arrived to help with the arrangements. The next to speak was a young mother, whose voice broke when she told how Margaret had rocked her sick baby so she could get a few hours sleep. A state patrol officer's wife spoke of how Margaret had ministered to her months after her husband's murder, when it seemed everyone else had forgotten her grief.

Father reclaimed the microphone. "Probably everyone here has a story to share," he said. "Margaret's prayers and small acts of loving service did not make headlines, but they made big differences in people's lives." Did we, he challenged us, make differences?

I couldn't meet Father's eyes—I felt like he was speaking directly to me. I focused on the flowers on the altar instead. I realized that I was like the owner of a floral shop, so proud of my visibility in the community that I had forgotten the flowers must be delivered in order to reach the people who need them.

A small group of Margaret's friends lined up with their bagpipes to play "Amazing Grace." I sang the words, "I once was blind, but now I see." I did see now—I could see that Margaret had delivered a lifelong message of love and kindness, and I hoped I could follow on her path.

Angels skip along the seashore picking up shells, kissing each one. Angels traipse through the galaxy, touching stars and dancing on planets. Angels waltz through the heavens, full of joy and worship, flowing with majesty, rhythm, and love.

THE FLOWER LADY

*F*lowering plants didn't show up on Earth until relatively late in the planet's life. Evolutionist Charles Darwin is said to have called flowers "an abominable mystery," because "they appeared so suddenly and spread so fast."

Lifelong gardener Margie McLean would say that flowers' real mystery is their ability to lift the human spirit.

She learned to grow towering irises and lush beds of roses as a child watching her grandmother tend the garden that grew next to their Midwest farmhouse.

When Margie moved to Atlanta, she planted a large garden and grew more flowers than she could have imagined back home. She planted more beds each year, and while the yard became a kaleidoscope of color, sweet fragrances perfumed the summer air.

Margie gave flowers to her neighbors, but that did not satisfy her urge to spread the joy the flowers brought her. One day, she hit on the notion of delivering blooms to a nearby nursing home. She arranged the flowers in bouquets just as a florist would. Nurses pointed her toward lonely residents who would appreciate the flowers. Margie stopped for a few minutes to visit as she made each delivery. Some understood that the flowers were from her; others imagined that they had come from loved ones. It didn't matter either way to Margie; the looks of pure joy on their faces were thanks enough.

The deliveries became a weekly ritual. Margie enclosed cards that addressed residents by name and included encouraging personal messages.

"Hope you're feeling better this week, Bert! Love, Margie" one card said.

"Thanks for your wonderful smile!" another card praised a gentleman who always appeared cheerful despite his many infirmities.

Nurses now alert the "Flower Lady," as residents call her, to bring special bouquets when a resident needs a lift.

Margie says, "There's nothing like a bouquet of flowers to show someone that he or she is loved."

"Angel" is the only word in the language
which can never be worn out.

—VICTOR HUGO, *LES MISÉRABLES*

RESCUED ON THE ROADSIDE

*H*ot and bitter. Prickly and sweaty. Alienated and full of self-pity. That's how I felt. It was summer in the Deep South, and I was standing on the side of an isolated two-lane road in the middle of nowhere with the flattest-looking tire I'd ever seen. It certainly hadn't been a good day. It hadn't even been a good year.

Sitting down on the edge of the backseat, looking out at the pastoral nothingness, I felt exhausted. Only the sight of my three-year-old son, Ian, sleeping in the car seat beside me provided any relief from the feelings that were overwhelming me. God was handing me one stinking, rotten deal after another. I knew my faith was being tested, and I was flunking the test.

I had set out on the ill-fated 200-mile round-trip drive for a job interview with new tires on my freshly tuned-up car. At least we would have a safe trip with no mishaps, I thought. Wrong. The interview hadn't even gone well. So now I was on my way back home to a low-paying newspaper job—assuming I could ever get back on the road. I enjoyed my job, but I was tired of eating cereal three meals a day, of constantly worrying about money, and of feeling so unbearably alone all the time. Everything was a challenge, from finding decent child care to paying for medical insurance. I was anxious, overextended, and desperate much of the time.

It seemed that the harder I tried, the further behind I got. I wanted a break.

I knew our situation wasn't much different from that of a lot of single-parent families. But I criticized myself for not doing well and then criticized myself for feeling bad about my failures. It was a downward emotional spiral.

I took a swig of water from the thermos I had prudently brought along. Then, after checking on my son, I got the spare, an inferior-looking piece of rubber, out of the trunk, along with the tire iron and the jack. I went to work on the lug nuts. My geriatric car had long since lost its hubcaps. I tried to turn the last rusty nut, but it wouldn't budge. I was getting sweatier and more aggravated. My hand slipped, and I scraped the skin entirely off the middle knuckle of my right hand. Blood gushed everywhere. I grabbed some tissues and applied direct pressure, trying to remember when I'd had my last tetanus shot.

I sat down next to Ian and gave in to my tears. It wasn't just the tire, the heat, and the bad interview—it was my whole pathetic life and, even worse, the life I was giving my son.

Cars zipped by, and no one stopped. I just sat and cried. I was so overwhelmed, I didn't even hear the people approach. I was startled when I heard a woman's soft voice asking, "Are you all right?"

I was embarrassed to be caught crying. "My tire's flat, and I can't get the lug nut off."

"What did you do to your hand?" asked a male voice. I looked up into a face that was so scarred it was hard for me to look at him.

"The tire," I said, pointing to the culprit.

"You got water?" he asked.

I told him I did. He reached for the thermos and poured the cool water over my hand, then gently wiped it with the tissue. Reaching into his wallet, he pulled out an adhesive bandage and placed it on my knuckle. Not a word passed between us the whole time.

The young woman looked at Ian, who was sleeping soundly. "He's a cutie," she said, smiling. She was pretty, with an open, vivacious face. "Waldo will fix your tire. He's good at mechanical things."

Waldo was already loosening the lug nut. If I hadn't been so hot and tired, I would have felt a little humiliated, but at that point I was too exhausted to care. My son stirred. As soon as he opened his eyes and spotted the smiling woman, he started grinning.

"Your spare's real bad. You need to get a new one real soon," Waldo said.

The woman identified herself as Laurie. She played patty-cake and peekaboo with a delighted Ian and made up wonderfully inventive stories to amuse him while Waldo finished his labors.

"You're all set," Waldo said, a beautiful smile brightening and softening his ravaged face.

"We've gotta go," Laurie said, waving good-bye to Ian. "It's almost time for supper, and then we've got church."

"About a mile down the road," Waldo told me, "there's a service station. My friend Billy works there, and he'll fix you up with a good tire cheap. You gotta replace the tire I put on and get a new spare, too. I'll call him from the house to let him know you're coming. You take care."

Waldo and Laurie ran off down the embankment toward a dilapidated mobile home park. Both of them turned and waved. I waved back.

When I got to the service station, Billy was waiting. He handed me a soda. "Waldo said to fix you up with a good used tire 'cause your spare's shot. I got one here I'll let you have for eight bucks. I won't charge you no labor on account of Waldo sending you." While he worked, he talked—Billy was a talker. He told me he had grown up with Waldo. They'd gone to Vietnam together. "He got hurt over there," Billy said. He took his greasy hands and made a circular motion over his face. "When he came back, he had to go through a lot of surgeries for his injuries. He was engaged to Laurie's sister, and she dumped him."

"And Laurie . . . ?" I asked.

"Well," he smiled, "we all used to kid him before the war about Laurie having a crush on him. He always laughed it off 'cause he'd been going with her sister since junior high. But when he came back, it was Laurie that was there for him. She visited him in the hospital. She read to him and sang songs for him. Then, when he got out, she drove him to his rehabilitation visits. Bit by bit, we all saw it coming—he just fell for that girl. They got married soon after." He stood up. "You're good to go."

I thanked Billy. He said he always takes care of anyone Waldo sends his way. I wondered how many people Waldo and Laurie have rescued. A man who carries bandages, and a young woman with a healing smile.

If ever you feel your arms are too short to reach for the heavens, fear not, for there is an angel reaching out to meet you halfway.

CHEERS FOR THE BUS DRIVER

Dorothy perches on the edge of the porch bench, feet gently tapping on the terra cotta bricks of the patio as she waits eagerly for her ride. It's Tuesday, and there should be a new delivery of peaches at her favorite farm stand. Thank goodness! With the church bake sale coming up in just a couple days, Dorothy had started to worry that she wouldn't be able to bake her renowned peach pie as she had done for more years than she cared to remember.

She sighs. Until she failed her driving test last year—at the age of 85!—she hadn't realized how dependent she was on her car. She used it to run errands, visit friends, and—especially—to drive across town to the movie theater. Dorothy tries to remember the last time she's been to a movie. She used to see almost every new release, but now it's been a while since she's seen any movie at all. When she lost her license, she lost more than the ability to drive. She also lost her independence—her freedom. She still has the energy to bake pies, go to the movies, and socialize with her friends, but she no longer has the means to do these things.

She sighs again, then begins to smile as she sees a familiar van pull around the corner and turn into her driveway. Anne waves and grins from behind the wheel. "Come on," she calls. "The movie starts in an hour, and Sean Connery's not going to wait around for you forever!"

Dorothy gathers her purse, straightens her hat, and starts carefully down the steps, grinning.

When Dorothy first met Anne through her church, she took an immediate liking to the energetic, friendly young woman. As their friendship developed, Dorothy began to recognize that Anne, who had never known her own grandparents, delighted in "adopting" surrogate grandparents. That was just fine with Dorothy, who already felt a strong tie to Anne.

When Anne saw Dorothy's despondence over losing her license, Anne got an idea. In no time, it seemed, she went to school and obtained a license permitting her to drive vans and even buses. Anne now uses this license to give joy to senior citizens, Dorothy included. Anne cheerfully chauffeurs her friends around on errands, but she also racks her brain to plan fun activities for them. Some of their favorite excursions have been to the local zoo, a doll museum, the beach, and the Botanic Gardens.

As Dorothy carefully steps into the van, ready for their outing—first to see the latest summer blockbuster and then on to the farm stand to take care of business—she reflects that Anne has been much more than a chauffeur for her. She is also her friend—her angel.

Angels give themselves fully,
for they have seen the face of love.

AN ELEPHANT NEVER FORGETS

My grandmother held that all of us, at least once in our lifetime, would encounter an angel in disguise. Mine came in the form of a 19-year-old mentally challenged woman dressed in a hospital housekeeper's uniform. Her name was Angie.

I was 22 when I met Angie. Seemingly healthy other than some swelling and a few pesky sores on my legs, I was hospitalized for tests. It took four months for doctors to diagnose an inflammation of my blood vessels caused by systemic lupus. This caused severe leg problems. My right leg was amputated, and I was left with nerve damage and deformity of my left leg and foot. Worse yet, as far as my vanity was concerned, I ballooned from a size 10 to a size 22 from massive steroid intake. The steroids also distorted my facial features and body shape. The crowning blow was the loss of my hair from aggressive chemotherapy. I'd stopped looking in the mirror to avoid gawking at the bald, bloated creature that stared back.

Only Angie seemed oblivious to the ravages of my illness. Every other visitor averted their eyes. Even nurses seemed to look anywhere but at me. My boyfriend, Mike, came less and less, finally fading away altogether. It seemed as though everyone I loved was deserting me. In my worst moments, I imagined God turning away also.

But Angie! My angel. The clinking of her massive key ring announced her arrival each morning.

"Hi," she greeted me daily. She'd walk straight to my bed and look directly at me with her huge brown eyes. "Are you better today?"

She asked with such utter sincerity and hope that I felt obligated to answer "a little better," even on my worst days. Angie would then grin and set about her tasks. While she worked, she shared stories about her mom, her sister, Lucy, and her pet cat, Boo. Before leaving the room, she never failed to ask if I needed anything.

One morning, during Angie's regular visiting time, I was on a stretcher in the hallway waiting for a ride to the operating room for a bone graft. I'd lost count of the number of such trips I had made in the past few months as surgeons struggled to save my remaining leg. I felt despondent and full of self-pity. God seemed farther away than ever.

As I lay staring at the wall, I felt a tap on my shoulder. There stood Angie, her face full of love and concern. She pressed something into my hand.

"You hold it," she said. "It always gives me the best luck."

She had placed a blue plastic elephant in my hand; it had always hung on her key ring.

"I won it at the fair," she said. "It's blue, just like your eyes."

I smiled. Through all my ailments and deformities, Angie saw the one part of me that had not changed—my eyes. She loved me the way God did—unconditionally. My spirits soared.

"Thanks, Angie," I said. "I'll take good care of it."

The blue elephant saw me through the surgery, then months of physical therapy and rehabilitation in a different hospital building. The grueling job of learning to live again took most of my time, but I found myself missing Angie. Once in a while, she would stop by my new room on her way home and visit for a few minutes before she had to leave to catch her bus. She always had a funny story about Boo's latest feline escapades. Those were my best days.

When the morning of my discharge finally arrived, Angie was right there. She insisted I keep the elephant. "So you'll remember me," she added.

I gave her a big hug. "I'll always remember you, Angie."

She grinned. "You're my friend. I'll remember you, too."

It would be an understatement to say that it was difficult to acclimate myself back into "normal" life, but I tried as hard as I could to keep my spirits up. Whenever I had a particularly trying day, or whenever I ached so much it was all I could do to drag my body out of bed, I would look at that blue plastic elephant and remember what Angie's friendship had given me.

Over the next few years, I sent notes and cards to Angie through the housekeeping department of the hospital. Then one day my letter was returned. Angie no longer worked there. She had moved with her family and left no forwarding address. But I still have contact with Angie through the little blue elephant that sits on my mantel.

No other gift will ever compare to this treasured gift of unconditional love from an angel in disguise.

Angels are the unseen hands that applaud you and the heavenly voices that cheer you on. All you have to do is listen and look with your heart.

SUZIE'S MINISTRY

*M*other's telephone rang at 6:45 A.M. as, I later learned, it does every morning.

She picked it up and said, "Good morning, Suzie." She listened a moment, said, "You, too," then hung up, smiling.

"Suzie who?" I asked.

"Mullens, only now it's Hightower."

Why was my little sister's best friend from high school calling Mother—especially so early? It didn't sound as if it were important. Their conversation was so brief.

Two of my adult siblings live in the metro area, but as busy days clip by and good intentions fall by the wayside, we out-of-towners, who must schedule our visits, usually see Mom more often than those who live nearby.

After Dad died three years ago, Mother talked a good game to us kids, saying she welcomed the opportunity to live alone since she never had. Even though she was beyond retirement age, she insisted on working part-time so she would continue to have other people in her life. She cultivated new interests, attended concerts and lectures, and signed up for short courses and night classes. I wasn't too concerned about her until she mentioned changing the lightbulb on the front porch.

"Did you use the kitchen step stool for a ladder?" I had a mental picture of her climbing, maybe losing her balance.

"No." Mother is evasive when she doesn't like the question.

"So, how did you get up there?"

"I'd like to eat Chinese tonight. Doesn't that sound good?"

I was wise to her tactics. "Mother, how did you change that lightbulb?"

"I used a chair. Now, does Bill like Chinese or not?"

"Yes. Chinese is fine. Which chair?" Glancing around, I didn't like the selection I saw. There was a wicker number in the entry hall, a wing chair, and an antique rocker in the living room.

"You are so nosy."

"Right. Which chair did you use?"

"The step stool is very steady."

Another dodge. "But you didn't bother to bring the step stool all the way from the kitchen, did you?"

She grimaced. "When is Bill going to be ready? We need to get going."

"Mother." I was getting exasperated. "Which chair?"

"The rocker, nosy; not that it's any of your business."

I shivered as I visualized her teetering under the light fix-ture on the front porch. "What if you had fallen?"

"I would have yelled for one of my neighbors."

Then I had a sudden, frightening thought. "What if you pulled a stunt like that inside the house and fell? You could be injured and suffer for days before anyone knew."

"Suzie would know."

"What does Suzie have to do with it?"

"She calls me every morning. If I'm going to be out, I turn on the answering machine so she knows I'm OK. But if there's no answer, she can be here in 15 minutes."

Bewildered, I couldn't help smiling. "Suzie calls you every morning to make sure you're all right?"

"Yes. She's an early riser, like me. She dials on the speaker phone while she fixes her boys their breakfast."

"What does she say?"

"I say, 'Good morning, Suzie,' she gives me a quick weather update, and then she tells me to have a nice day. It just takes a minute."

I've always liked Suzie, but suddenly I had a new regard for her. "How did she happen to start calling you?"

"I went to her dad's funeral a couple years ago, and appar-ently she had started calling her mother each morning while he was in the hospital. She asked if I'd mind if she checked in on me in the mornings, too."

Mom explained, "I enjoy living alone, keeping my own hours. But in the back of my mind, I was a little concerned that something might happen sometime and no one would know. Since Suzie started calling, I don't worry about it."

Mother wasn't the only one who felt relieved.

Suzie's calls aren't specifically suggested in scripture, other than the general "Love thy neighbor," and I've never heard a sermon that mentioned anything like this. It seems Suzie has created a ministry of her own. It's a unique service and, with families scattered all over the country, younger friends looking out for older friends seems like a great idea.

I thought of the elderly acquaintances in my hometown whose families live far away, and I realized that there were a couple of possibilities for my own version of Suzie's ministry. I still wasn't happy about Mom using the rocker as a step stool, but I felt much better knowing there was someone checking in on her every day. And if I could help give someone else that peace of mind, then Suzie's ministry will have been doubly successful.

Angels surround our lives with love and protection. Know that they are among us to ease our burdens, shield us from evil, lighten our hearts, and guide us along our journey.

GUARDIAN ANGELS

One day when we face these beings of light who have guided our paths and done God's work in our lives, we will wonder how we ever overlooked their presence.

❧❧❧

A BIG MAN

*I*ce—huge chunks that could punch holes in a boat's bow or shove it wrecked against the shore—threatened traffic on the Mississippi River that frigid night. Cargoes, boats, and whole crews had been known to become lost in conditions like these. But people whose livelihoods are tied to the river tried not to think about the worst. Lights scanned the black waters ahead, and pilots strained to see. Ice warnings were radioed to all boats within hearing distance, and tensions ran high.

In better weather, old boats, permanently moored and set up as supply stations at ports along the river, broadcast information on conditions. But tonight the ice threatened even those vessels, and most operators shut down and went ashore. Captains held their breath approaching the Mississippi's treacherous junction with the Ohio River. If only they knew what to expect!

Just when each captain had resigned to navigating the passage blind, a deep, reassuring baritone crackled over the radio: "Downbound... any downbound boats. This is Cairo supply station." It was the operator that river men had nicknamed "Big Voice," renowned for his powerful voice and his meticulous reports on river conditions. He was still on the air!

Captains almost leapt for joy, not quite able to believe that Big Voice hadn't abandoned his old boat and headed for safety.

With calm authority, Big Voice described a narrow passage through the massing ice, relaying reports from boats that had already made the run.

The night wore on, and Big Voice kept broadcasting. He was a lifeline for the half-dozen boats and their crews that were attempting to navigate the treacherous junction. When he suddenly lost touch with one boat, Big Voice radioed for rescue crews and then announced triumphantly over the air that the crew had been plucked from the freezing water.

As dawn broke gray and dim, signaling an end to the boaters' ordeal, the voice went silent. Grateful captains assumed that Big Voice had signed off for some much-deserved rest.

A few hours later, the captain of the boat that had wrecked went in search of Big Voice, intending to thank him for his help. The captain discovered the old vessel shoved onto shore, with a jagged tear in its bow; it was tilting precariously toward the raging, icy river. Before long, the old junker would plunge into the river and sink. The captain hesitated to board the foundering craft—surely anyone on board would have disembarked by now. But something told him he should take a look around. He carefully made his way onto the boat, his steps tentative on the icy deck, his hands stretched blindly in front of him as he groped for a safe hold.

"Hello!" he called into the dark interior. "Anyone on board?"

"Over here. I'm over here!" The captain recognized the voice. Puzzled, he threaded his way through the dim, murky interior.

"Over here, behind the desk," the voice said. "Lucky you showed up. I sure could use some help."

The captain peered over the desk, and tears sprang to his eyes at what he saw. A wheelchair lay overturned, and a frail young man, not more than 20 years old, had pulled himself up on one arm and was struggling into a sitting position, dragging withered legs.

"You're Big Voice!" the captain exclaimed.

"I guess that's what they call me," the young man answered, looking embarrassed. "I guess some ice hit the boat, and I was knocked out of my chair. I'm sorry I couldn't stay on the air longer."

"You're helpless on a sinking boat, and you're worried about us out there," the captain said, shaking his head in wonder. He righted the chair and lifted the shivering young man, wrapping a blanket around him. "I've been on the river most of my life—in plenty of bad spots, worse even than last night—but you make me feel small, son. You make me feel small."

For He will command His angels concerning you
to guard you in all your ways.

—PSALM 91:11

A Doctor's Promise

*W*earing a white medical coat with his name on the pocket, Dr. Ronald Greene, a stocky man who looked to be in his sixties, greeted me in his Chicago office on a warm June day in 1958. A fringe of white hair framed his head. He wore glasses—and a huge smile.

"Your first baby?" he asked.

"Yes."

"Sit down, please, and tell me about yourself." He sat at his desk, his bright eyes looking into mine.

I explained that I worked as a secretary and that my husband and I had moved to Chicago so he could attend Northwestern Dental School in the fall.

Dr. Greene glanced at the patient information chart I had filled out. "You live on Kenmore. That's near Wrigley Field, isn't it?"

I nodded.

"I love watching the Cubs. Have you seen them play?"

I shook my head. "Not yet."

He chuckled. "That's one place struggling students can go on the cheap." He sighed. "I think back to when I was in med school more years ago than I care to remember. Learned to live on a shoestring." He paused. "Tuition has skyrocketed since my day. How do you manage?"

"Until school starts, Don's working days as a chemist at Industrial Adhesives and nights at Banker's Life & Casualty. I work for Blue Shield."

As I talked, Dr. Greene made notes on my chart.

"No relatives in the area?"

I shook my head. "No."

"Home phone?"

"Not yet, but we'll be getting a phone in a couple of months. We can be reached at the work numbers."

"Well, young lady," he said, "my nurse will give you a gown for the exam, and then we'll talk about what to expect during your pregnancy. I'll answer any questions you might have. All right?"

I hesitated for just a moment. Dr. Greene must have sensed what I needed to know.

"You have Blue Shield, right?"

I nodded. "It's an 80/20 plan."

"Good. I'm charging half my usual fee," he said. "Whatever your insurance pays will cover everything."

Tears gathered in my eyes. I knew that Dr. Greene had a reputation for being one of the best obstetricians in Chicago and was widely respected as a researcher and as a doctor. "That doesn't sound like enough, Dr. Greene."

He winked and grinned. "Help someone else when you can," he said. "Besides, I love bringing babies into the world."

I kept each appointment faithfully. The nausea disappeared in a few weeks, and except for being exhausted some days after work, I felt wonderful! I wrote weekly letters to my mother and mother-in-law, sharing my excitement and my joy. How I wished that my mother lived in Chicago instead of in Utah! Still, I made friends in the community and in the church, some of whom were also expectant moms.

Shortly before my due date, I went in to Dr. Greene's office for a routine checkup. "The baby hasn't dropped yet," he said. "You have another week to ten days before delivery."

My baby had other plans. Riding home in our car with my husband's carpool buddies, my water broke.

"I think we'd better hurry home," I said. "We need to call Dr. Greene and get back to the hospital."

An intern met us at the door. "The doctor needs X rays," he said, rushing me down the hall. "He's on his way."

Thirty minutes later Dr. Greene arrived. I had no labor pains. Not one.

"Your baby's head is pinching the umbilical cord," he said. "The greenish-brown amniotic fluid is a signal that the baby is in distress. I need to do an emergency C-section—right now!"

My back burned when the anesthesiologist gave me a spinal, but during the surgery I felt only pressure, no pain. I heard voices as Dr. Greene delivered the baby and worked to get him to breathe. I waited. My heart all but stopped. Silence. Then, a baby's cry!

"It's a beautiful boy!" Dr. Greene said in a choked voice, holding Michael close so I could see him. Tears glistened in his eyes. "That was a close call."

Dr. Greene insisted on a ten-day hospital stay. He knew I would be on my own once I left the hospital, since Don was in school and holding down two jobs. He ordered me not to climb the steep stairs to our second-story apartment for two weeks—after Don helped me the first time—and to keep in touch by phone. I followed his instructions explicitly.

A month later, I was back in Dr. Greene's office with Michael for my final checkup. "Dr. Greene," I said, opening my purse, "I know you hadn't counted on a C-section when you quoted me your price for delivering the baby. Don and I want . . ."

He closed my purse and took my hand in his. "Remember what I told you on your first visit?" he said gently. "Life isn't about money—it's about helping others. Do that, and I will have been repaid many times over." He smiled that gentle smile. "Promise?"

"Yes, I promise."

Many years have passed since I made that promise back in 1958, and Dr. Ronald Greene has long since left us. Yet, each time I anonymously give a scholarship, pick up a restaurant tab for an elderly couple, slip a $20 bill into the hand of a stranger in need, or share my time, encouragement, and love with someone struggling along life's road, I think about my promise and see a kindly doctor smiling down from the heavens.

**Reach out to someone in need,
and one day they might call you "Angel."**

Mrs. Trapp's Tenderness

*L*eslie was pouty and selfish, as I recall from my kinder-garten days. At least, she started out that way. No one, absolutely no one, wanted to be her friend within the first week of school. We didn't really know much about her, but no one wanted to get to know her better.

I don't know how long Mrs. Trapp had taught, but she was well into her sixties when I was her student. And she was as patient an educator as I would ever meet.

Each morning, Mrs. Trapp would select a new VIP for the day. That student chose a helper to unfold the flag and lead the class in the Pledge of Allegiance. The VIP was also commissioned to take his or her partner down to the cafeteria's kitchen to carry up trays of cookies and milk for snack time. It was a coveted honor, and the VIP always chose his or her best friend as a helper.

When my day to be VIP came around for the second time that year, I was fully prepared to select my partner. But before I could, Mrs. Trapp took me aside and whispered something utterly unimaginable in my ear. "Will you pick Leslie?" she asked.

"Why?" I asked incredulously. Her answer came with a pleading look of concern and compassion: "Leslie needs a friend."

I understood, but it was still painful to call out, "I choose Leslie."

Mrs. Trapp's mission to melt Leslie's hostility was underway. First, Leslie looked around in disbelief, but because everyone was looking back at her, she realized that she had heard correctly. "Me?" she squealed and bounded to the front of the room.

As the day progressed, I noticed that Leslie was trying hard to be nice. Mrs. Trapp's plan was already taking effect. I'd like to say it was an overnight success, but it wasn't. It took many weeks before Leslie established friendships with her classmates. But by the time the school year was over, she was one of us.

Last I heard, Mrs. Trapp, then in her nineties, had been recently honored at a special celebration for her many years of service in education. Though I learned my ABCs from her, I'll always remember her more for the TLC she gave to all of us.

Angels carry messages from heaven to earth.
God uses his angels to tell us of his mercy and
to show us the way he wants us to go.

THE BLUE SCARF

I was 16 when my Aunt Emily became so crippled with arthritis that it was difficult for her to get out much. My mom suggested that I earn some extra money by doing her shopping for her. I, as a busy teenager, felt I had more important things to do, and I told Mom that Emily could probably find someone else to help her. My mom tried to explain to me about families helping each other out, but it fell on deaf ears. I barely even knew Emily. She and her husband had moved back into town only a few years before, and I had seen them on only a handful of occasions before he suddenly died.

I'm ashamed now to admit that two of my best friends lived quite near Aunt Emily, and I used to avoid passing her house when I'd go to visit them. That way she couldn't see me and call for me to help her. At the time, I felt very little guilt about this. Emily might be my mom's sister, but I hardly knew her. I had my own life to lead—she was simply not a part of it.

But later that spring, when the new fashions were coming out and I had no money to buy them, I asked Mom if Emily had found someone to help her out. She said that a lady did Emily's shopping, and she managed most of her cleaning herself with some help from Mom. I admitted that I needed money, so I offered to help.

I went to see Emily, and she had a list all ready for me. I did her shopping for a few weeks, sometimes taking a friend along with me. Emily always offered us cookies and said how grateful she was.

One day my friend Anna and I were at Emily's house, waiting for her to finish her shopping list. Anna noticed my blue scarf and remarked, "Oh, I wish I'd known you had that—it matches the dress I wore last Saturday!"

I shrugged. "You can borrow it whenever you want to."

My aunt said casually, "If you girls shared things like that, you could save money."

We looked at her, and she said, "You could keep all your unusual accessories at someone's house, and maybe earrings and shoes, too."

Anna and I talked about her idea while we shopped, and then we discussed it with another friend. It really did make sense. Anna had gold nail polish she didn't use much, and I had a new gold top; Janice had red shoes that she only wore with one outfit, and Anna and I were both eager to try them on.

Janice, Anna, and I went back to Aunt Emily's with her groceries, and we were still buzzing about her idea. Emily heard us talking and casually offered, "If you'd like, you could keep your things here. You live so close, it would be very convenient, and I have a nice-size spare room that you could use."

We eagerly accepted her offer, and brought over scarves and shoes, then belts and handbags and even clothes. Before we went out for an evening, we would all stop by Emily's to try on various outfits and accessories. A full-length mirror appeared in the room, and Emily would offer us cans of soda. And when we brought back what we had worn, Emily would ask about our evening out. We soon began to confide in her, telling her things we didn't even tell our moms.

We soon got to know Emily as a warm and interesting person. She told us about the crazy things she and her husband, Bill, had done when they were young.

When we all went off to college, we still kept in touch with Emily, sending her postcards and always dropping by when we were home on vacation. Eventually, we could see that she was getting more frail.

One day, Emily fell trying to reach a pitcher on a high shelf in her kitchen. She was rushed to the hospital, where she died the next day—the doctors said she'd had a heart attack. When mom called Anna and me to tell us the news, both of us cried at the loss of our friend.

All of us girls who had used Emily's as our "changing room" met up for her funeral. It was the first great loss any of us had ever had, and it was awful. We went back to our house after the funeral, and my mom said, "I have something for each of you from Emily." She handed out identical packages to us. We opened them to find a blue scarf and the same note in each.

"If it wasn't for the blue scarf, all of us would have missed out on our special friendship. Love, Emily."

That was ten years ago, and now I'm married with children of my own. My husband, Eric, and I travel frequently, bringing back many lovely souvenirs and keepsakes. But to this day, the special spot on my bedroom dressing table is home to my little blue scarf. I have never worn it, and I never will. For me, it's a reminder to reach out to people. And it's a reminder of Emily.

When someone we love passes from mortality,
it eases the pain to realize we have not lost a friend,
but we have gained an angel.

ROCK-A-BYE BABY

I was pumping as high as I dared in the white wicker swing on our sprawling front porch that sultry Southern summer afternoon. The air was fragrant with frothy pink mimosa blossoms and freshly mowed grass. Steam rose from the puddles that dusty birds dipped and splashed in.

I was serving as lookout for the cousins' arrival.

They were driving all the way from New Mexico to a family reunion this evening here at our house in the East Tennessee hills.

There had been a lot of "tsk-tsking" and head shaking from my grandmother, my mother, and my aunts when the southwestern relatives had announced they would be driving to the reunion. There was another baby on the way for their family. Number five.

I was too young to understand that cross-country trips and babies on the way didn't mix well. All I knew was that it sounded like an adventure to me. I hadn't been out of the state of Tennessee in my whole eight years of life.

The time of arrival came and went.

No one, though, really thought much about it. My family was known for showing up with seconds to spare for weddings, funerals, school, church. The preacher had even gotten to where he checked to see if we were seated before he started in. I figured he'd gotten tired of being upstaged as we traipsed in trying to be quiet.

Soon, though, the entire family joined me on the front porch, chasing stray breezes.

All the cooking was done, right down to having the lemons squeezed, the mint ready to toss into it. The fried chicken was being kept warm, and the biscuits were just waiting to be mixed up and popped in the oven. My mouth watered.

The telephone rang.

Mama answered it with a question in her voice. "Hello?"

After a pause that was longer than necessary to tell us they would be just a little late, Mama said, "Thank God."

"There's been an accident," she turned to say, covering the receiver with her hand. "No one is hurt. They're taking tests to make sure the baby is OK."

Later that afternoon, in my bath towel/Superman cape, I was standing on the porch railing when the cousins' car finally turned the corner.

I let out a hoop 'n' a holler, and everyone came running just as the cousins pulled up in a rented car. I could tell it was rented because there was no dent in the passenger side and no broken headlights, no mangled tires. That was all the detail Mama had been able to get from my uncle.

The four children, the cousins I'd been waiting for, clambered from the car and ran into our waiting arms. My Aunt Callie was the last one to step from the car, holding onto my uncle's arm. And then, to my utter astonishment, he turned back and gently lifted a black-and-white dog from the front seat. Its leg was bandaged, and the dog hobbled a bit when Uncle Willie set it down on the grass.

It looked up questioningly at my aunt. "Come on," she said to the dog, stooping awkwardly to stroke its back. "I want you to meet your family." She turned to us. "This little fella has a story to tell," she proclaimed.

"Let's eat first," Mama said, worrying about the chicken and roast beef in the oven, the ice melting in the lemonade.

Aunt Callie smiled. "The story will keep," she said. Uncle Willie carefully carried the pup to the porch, where he served him the first slice of beef—on a real dinner plate, much to Mama's displeasure. But Mama didn't say anything, just clamped her mouth shut like she does sometimes.

The rest of the evening passed in a blur of " . . . pass the chicken, coleslaw, potato salad, biscuits, strawberry jam." After a while we cut into the watermelon and followed it with a seed-spitting contest. I came in second.

We didn't get around to hearing the rest of the story about the dog until after supper, when everyone was sitting on the porch taking turns cranking the ice-cream freezers. The dog lay, one eye open, at my aunt's feet. The squeak of the twin rocking chairs where my grandparents sat was accompanied by the swishing of lawn sprinklers; lightning bugs flickered on the distant hillside.

"There we were, making good time even with a steady hard rain and all the potty stops," my Aunt Callie said, beginning the tale.

"And then all of a sudden she shouted, 'STOP!'" said Uncle Willie, picking up the story.

"A black-and-white dog," he continued, "was standing right in the middle of the road not two car lengths away."

As one, we all stared at the dog, finally sleeping soundly, apparently oblivious to our interest.

Uncle Willie, according to the story as it unfolded, pulled the station wagon off the highway and, at Aunt Callie's insistence, went back to see if the dog was OK. It followed him back to the car, jumped in, and settled on Callie's lap.

"Licking my hand, as if to say 'Thanks,' it turned in a circle and went to sleep right there in my lap!" Aunt Callie said.

Speechless, she and Uncle Willie had looked at one another. But they were already running late and didn't have time to find an animal shelter.

"We neither one had the heart to leave the dog on the highway," volunteered Uncle Willie, pausing to take a sip of lemonade.

"The baby seemed to like the dog sitting so close," Aunt Callie said, rubbing her stomach now. "This little baby stretched out a tiny foot right at the dog lying next to it until I knew it could feel it! That's when I told Willie that it looked to me like we were going to have a new baby *and* a new pet!"

They were laughing about that when a truck ran a stop sign and rammed into their station wagon.

The dog crashed into the dashboard and was pinned there from the force of the collision. It suffered a broken leg but was mostly just bruised all over.

"The baby, thank heaven," Aunt Callie said, rubbing the roundness of her stomach, "was just fine." She hesitated a moment, looking at Uncle Willie, then swallowed hard like she had a piece of biscuit stuck in her throat. "The doctors said that the dog cushioned the impact of the accident and saved the baby's life."

"So do you know what we named this sweet ol' dog?" Uncle Willie asked, reaching for Aunt Callie's hand.

"Michael, of course, for the angel."

God committed the care of men and all things
under heaven to Angels.

—JUSTIN MARTYR

NIGHT-LIGHT

*I*t had been a mistake to come to the cabin. It was too soon. It had been only six months since Dorothy's death—not nearly long enough to ease Marc's pain. But it was Memorial Day weekend, and he could think of no place he'd rather be.

Just driving down the dirt road sent him bouncing back in time. They'd bounced along it together years ago hoping to hasten the baby's arrival. How they'd laughed when Steven was born that very night.

The pine tree by the bend in the road brought tears to his eyes. He shook his head to make them go away. He remembered he'd shaken his head at their naïveté when, years ago, they brought their potted Christmas tree to plant beside their mountain retreat. Neither of them had realized it would be impossible to dig in the frozen January ground. They brought the tree back the next spring. It had been smaller than little Sarah then. Now it towered above his head. He'd wanted Dorothy to see it last winter, but she'd been too weak, the cancer too advanced.

Where had the time gone? Somehow their 33 years of marriage seemed shorter than their last six months together. He could see the flannel nightgown Dorothy had been wearing that last morning of her life more clearly than the beautiful tulle dress she'd worn on their wedding day. The memory of the night-light he kept on so she wouldn't be frightened when she woke in pain eclipsed his memory of the lighthouse night-light they had picked out for the kids while vacationing in Cape Cod. The names of the hospice volunteers came to his mind more quickly than the names of their lifelong friends.

Marc opened the cabin door. The smell of the potpourri she made last summer overwhelmed him. She'd dried the flowers just days before the doctor gave them the dire prognosis. Inoperable, incurable, inescapable.

Dorothy's death had been a blessing. That's what everyone said. She was so brave ... only begging for mercy and medication at the very end when the pain was no longer bearable. It wasn't until then that he'd ever thought, even for a moment, that her dying might be preferable to her living.

Marc dropped onto the couch in front of the wood-burning stove. They had sat in front of it together for the last time when they came up in early September to see the aspens. The bright green leaves of summer had already started to change to the color of copper pennies. Even then he realized Dorothy was changing too, moving away from her earthly life.

He laid a fire. If he could force himself to stay the weekend he would need it for warmth. Nights were always cold in the Rockies. Marc could even remember one Memorial Day weekend when it had snowed. He and Dorothy and the kids roasted marshmallows and played a marathon game of Monopoly. They snuggled together that night beneath several layers of blankets.

Suddenly Marc shook himself. Enough! He knew he had to get out of the cabin. Grabbing the old denim jacket from the coat rack, he plunged out the door. He headed down the river to Horizon Point, a high, steep peak with a panoramic view.

Marc started his upward climb, his footsteps heavy, his heart even heavier. Almost unconsciously he began making a plan. He could "accidentally" fall from the top. Every summer one or two people lost their lives climbing in the Rockies. He had left no note, and he'd never mentioned suicide, so no one would be the wiser. By the time he approached the tree line, rain splatted on the rocks beside him. So much the better, he thought. People would think he had slipped.

The temperature was dropping rapidly, and the rain was mixing with snow. What a release death would be. He wouldn't have to endure the loneliness any longer. As he trudged upward, he remembered the times he led the family on this very same hike. "Our fearless leader," Dorothy had teased.

The thought made him stop in his tracks. A fearless leader? Leaders don't trudge up the mountainside with no intention of returning. Leaders learn to go on, to make the most of what they have.

And how horrified Dorothy would be. Her last words had been, "Love the kids for both of us." Marc was suddenly ashamed. How could he ever have thought of ignoring Dorothy's dying wish? He'd been selfish to think only of himself. He wasn't the only one in pain—Steven and Sarah had lost their mother. They needed him.

Suddenly aware of the cold for the first time, Marc buttoned his jacket. It had been stupid to go climbing at this time of year without warmer clothing.

Snow swirled around him. The path disappeared. Disoriented, he paused to think. He had to get back to the cabin somehow. He'd freeze if he stayed on the mountain. He knew he needed to head down, but where was down? If he went the wrong way, he might fall from the cliff that rose above the river. The choice of living or dying no longer seemed his to make.

He inched his way over the rocks, hoping he was still on the trail. Then, peering through the snow and the late afternoon darkness, straining to catch his bearings, he thought he saw a light. It couldn't be from the cabin. He hadn't turned the lights on. Still, with no other options, he decided he'd head for it.

Cautiously he descended until he reached the shelter of the trees. He saw that he was on the trail. Hallelujah! He breathed a sigh of relief. As he followed it back to the cabin, he realized that the light that had guided him through the darkness was coming from his car.

On closer inspection, he discovered that his seat belt had caught in the car door and prevented it from closing completely. With the door held open, the dome light remained on, shedding just enough light to guide his journey down the mountain.

He thought of the night-light he'd always left on for Dorothy, and he smiled. Maybe God turned on night-lights, too.

Do they sit and watch us, these angels
of which we are unaware? Do they lie on a cloud,
heads on their hands, and peek at our world?
I think I can see them sometimes if I look up and
squint really hard. I think I can hear them sometimes,
celestial murmurs that accompany our hardships
and will one day lead us home.

THE STRANGER AT THE DOOR

*T*hroughout my youth, I watched as my father and his siblings always welcomed an opportunity to help someone in need. One day I mentioned this to my grandfather, and he replied, "They were helped when they were very young, so the least they can do is share their blessings with others." My grandfather sat back in his recliner—a sure sign he was about to deliver a great story. . . .

"I was what you'd call an adventurous fellow in my day. Life was exciting, and opportunities seemed to abound for those who liked a challenge. But I married young and had to settle down, much to the sorrow of my pals. Joe, the real daredevil of the group, headed west to seek his fortune—in those days, Ohio was considered the west. His was a daring journey, with no turnpikes or any of the other roadside conveniences we have now.

"Several months after Joe headed west, I got a letter from him proclaiming his great regret that I had been foolish enough to get married so young and find myself tied down now with seven children. If not for my growing family, I could have joined him in Ohio, which he described as 'the land of milk and honey.'

"Apparently Joe had not counted on my reaction to his letter. I couldn't think of any reason why I couldn't pack up my family and go west, too. But when I arrived, the opportunities weren't as plentiful as Joe had said. And by then he had moved even farther west.

"With our funds dwindling, we couldn't follow Joe or even return home. We settled down in an old deserted house, which the local people thought was haunted. Day after day I looked for work of any kind, but times were bad and no one had any idea whether or not I would stick around.

"Your grandmother and I ate very sparingly, saving most of our food for the children. Even so, we reached the point of not having enough food even for them. Fortunately, the children always accepted any changes that came their way, so they readily agreed to my proposal that we do things a little differently one night. Since we were all tired and cold, I suggested that we circle around the stove in the kitchen, kneel down and say our evening prayers, then rush to bed. We would eat, I assured them, when we woke up.

"Shortly after midnight, we heard a pounding on the front door. When I opened the door, there stood a stranger with a huge basket of food. He seemed as surprised to see me as I was to see him, or perhaps it was the sight of so many wide-eyed children coming down the steps that gave him a shock. In any event, he said he was delighted to find people living in this house, because his wife would never let him hear the end of it if his trip had been in vain. "He went on to say that each time he had fallen asleep that night, he'd heard a voice directing him to take food to the haunted house in the village. His wife told him it was only a dream and that if the neighbors saw him going out into the night loaded up with bags of groceries, they would think he was as crazy as a loon. Twice she persuaded him to go back to sleep, but when he heard the directive a third time, he got dressed and, despite his wife's jeering, loaded up all kinds of food and went out into the night."

Grandpa seemed rather shaken as he spoke of the experience. After a moment, he went on to say, "Now my children are grown and have children of their own. I hope they tell them about the stranger who came to our rescue that winter night. God works in mysterious ways. Perhaps someday they may be the instruments God uses to answer someone else's evening prayers."

If you pray truly, you will feel within yourself a great assurance, and the angels will be your companions.

—EVAGRIUS OF PONTUS,
SEASON OF THE SPIRIT

SYLVIA'S GUARDIAN ANGEL

ylvia is a nurse who works in a psychiatric ward at the local hospital. I got to know her when she enlisted my help in setting up her computer. Occasionally after that I did some typing on small administrative projects for her.

I had not seen Sylvia for several months. One evening I was riding home from work on my bicycle, pedaling fast because I was in a hurry. For some reason, I took a different route home, one that passed by Sylvia's street. When I reached Sylvia's building I had a sudden and inexplicable urge to stop. Something inside me said, "*Go see Sylvia.*"

Puzzled at the intensity of this feeling, I pulled the bicycle over to the sidewalk and hesitated. "First of all, she isn't even home," I told myself. "She works from 3:00 to 11:00, and it's after 6:00 now. She won't even be there." I started pedaling toward home, but there it was again, that silent, insistent urging: *Go see Sylvia.*

I decided I better follow through with the urge. If God was nudging me to do something, I figured there must be a reason for it. I pulled up in front of Sylvia's building, parked and locked my bike, and walked up the steps to Sylvia's door. I knocked three times. There was no answer.

"There, you see, it was nothing," I told myself, feeling foolish. I turned around to leave.

But just then I heard muffled footsteps, and the door opened slowly. There was Sylvia, wearing a wrinkled bathrobe, looking thin and as pale as a ghost. She had just come home from the hospital, she said, where she had almost died. She had pneumonia and a cold and was convalescing. She dabbed at her runny, red nose with a tissue, coughing and sniffling. She invited me to come in and have some tea.

As I helped her to the couch, I realized that a strong smell of gas permeated the rooms, so strong that my eyes started burning. I went to the kitchen and discovered that the gas on one of the burners was turned on but no flames were coming out.

Sylvia could not smell the gas fumes because of her cold.

I learned that a neighbor had dropped by a half hour earlier to heat up some soup for Sylvia's dinner. The neighbor had neglected to turn off the gas. I now turned the gas off, opened the windows, and got Sylvia out into the hallway.

I don't know what would have happened that day if God hadn't urged me to stop and see Sylvia. Would she have died of asphyxiation? Would the gas stove have eventually exploded and the apartment gone up in flames? It is not likely anyone would have checked on her after the neighbor left, certainly not until the next day.

Sylvia jokes and says maybe it was her guardian angel who saved her.

Perhaps.

She says her angel that day was me.

I don't know if I was enlisted as a guardian angel that day or not. But I do know that whenever I feel some kind of urging now, even if it seems odd or unreasonable at the time, I follow through with it. Sometimes—as in the instance with Sylvia—I know right away why I was "nudged." In other cases, I might never know.

So be prepared—who knows when God might call upon you to be someone's guardian angel.

There are many things in life we cannot see or hear or touch, but we know they exist because the heart tells us so. For the heart possesses a wisdom far beyond that of the intellect and a vision far grander than that of the mind.

GUIDING LIGHTS

*W*henever my sailor husband was assigned to sea duty, I would stay with my mother in Brownwood, Texas. During one such visit in 1954, we drove to a family reunion with my two daughters, Faye, three years old, and Sissie, almost two. When the reunion ended, the weather looked stormy, but we decided to head home anyway.

The highway took us through small towns and rural areas of Texas. Momma wanted to stop at Wiley, the all-black college where I received my degree in biology in 1947. To pay for my schooling, Momma had worked as a pastry chef, and Wiley was a monument of sorts to the years she spent baking hundreds of pies, cakes, and cookies.

But we had a ten-hour drive ahead of us, and dark clouds were gathering. The temperature was falling, so we stopped to put sweaters on the girls, and Momma sat in the backseat between them. Opening the box of sandwiches we had brought along, she passed one to me and said, "Don't worry about us. We're as warm as toast."

But I was worried. It was hard for me to see. If I had known then that I had night blindness, I would have tried to find a place to stop. But being black meant that we could not just pull into a motel and wait out the storm. Segregation still prevailed.

When night came, the falling snow curtained off the sky. Even the moon and stars were invisible. When I pulled into a truck stop to get gas, I told the station attendant that I could scarcely see the road. He was concerned when he realized I intended to keep driving.

Foolishly, I got back in the car with my mother and my two babies and started out again. I soon realized I could not see the road. It was as though we were in a dark cave, and I began to panic. I couldn't see to go forward; I couldn't see to turn around. Pulling off to the side of the road was out of the question, as I could not see that either. I wasn't even sure that I was on the road!

I tried to pray, but I was almost paralyzed with fear. Briefly, I put my head on the steering wheel and rubbed my eyes in hopes of seeing better. When I looked up, I saw lights approaching in the rearview mirror. The lights turned out to be from two 18-wheelers. One drove around in front of my car and slowed down. The other stayed behind us, its lights casting a welcome glow inside the car. I knew in my heart that the man at the gas station had told those truckers about my predicament, and they had decided to help. God had answered the prayer I could not utter.

I nestled between the hovering vehicles like a chick taking refuge under its mother's wings. We traveled for some time this way, and then I saw the right-turn signal light blinking on the leading truck. The driver flashed his headlights several times as a way of saying good-bye before he turned onto another road. For a moment I was terrified to be back in the darkness, but then the truck that had been behind me pulled out in front and continued to act as my guide.

It was dawn when we finally got back to Brownwood. I blew my horn and waved at the trucker. He lowered his window and smiled as he waved back. I never knew the names of those drivers who helped deliver us safely home, but I will be forever grateful for the help they gave us on that dark night.

Guard me,

guide me, angels,

hide me from the troubles

all around.

Keep me safe and

give me faith to hear your steps

in every sound.

—A BEDTIME PRAYER

COMFORTING ANGELS

Because they've seen a better place, angels whisper hope to us in our darkest moments.

❧〜❧〜❧

MAY DAY

Time. There's just too much of it in here. Yet Brenda could remember when she seemed never to have enough time. Of course, that was before, when she had bustled through the full days and nights of motherhood and normalcy. The comparison—of then and now—gave new meaning to the phrase "once upon a time!"

And I'm sick and tired of being on a schedule.

Schedule, not routine. Routine was different. Routine meant fixing breakfast in the morning. Routine meant giving her husband a kiss along with his sack lunch each day. A schedule, though, meant being bathed each morning at 10:00. Being turned three times each shift to prevent bedsores. Or even being diapered—as regular as clockwork—every time you were, well, regular.

Brenda groaned inwardly at her clever play on words, something she'd always been good at. *Something I AM good at,* she corrected herself. *Maybe the only thing I'm still good at. People used to admire my quick wit.*

And she still had it. Only, no one knew but her. Even now, like this, she was something more than IV feedings, more than a nurse's duty, more than a wasted body. Did anyone remember that? Did God?

Are you listening, God? Or can't you hear me think over the hum of this respirator?

Why, Brenda could hardly hear herself think. The rhythmic hiss and underlying drone of the oxygen muffled each and every sound. It insulated her. Irritated her. Isolated her.

I despise being so helpless.

That's what the advanced stages of MS had done. The disease was a demon that stripped you of both your dignity and your choices. Like a thief in the night, multiple sclerosis sneaked in to rob you of one treasure after another: sensation, dexterity, range of motion, coordination, strength. Now, at 53, Brenda found herself as helpless as a baby—worse, even. At least an infant had a voice to indicate its needs.

I miss so much.

Brenda could remember (after all, she had lots and lots of time to remember) her favorite activity: traipsing through the woods after a fresh rain. She recalled how it made the soil cocoa-rich and how the breeze was as crisp and clean as a new dollar bill. She loved how the rain left everything smelling as sweet as a freshly bathed baby.

I feel so deserted, God. So alone. I'm not certain you're even there anymore. Are you, God? Are you there?

In the waning evening light, Brenda let her gaze slide around her room at Front Range Manor. She focused on the wall-to-wall photos tacked up by good-hearted, well-meaning friends and family. On days like today, the pictures were piercing reminders of a life she didn't have . . . couldn't have . . . wouldn't have.

Plump tears leaked down her cheeks, and she was too helpless even to wipe them away. She closed her eyes.

"Brenda," hesitantly.

"Brenda," louder.

"Brenda, are you awake?"

Brenda tediously twisted her mouth to form a guttural answer. "Wha . . . aaa . . . ahh?"

"Today is the first of May, Brenda. May Day, and I wanted to share it with you. Here, smell."

Even with her eyes closed, Brenda recognized the spring-time scent of lilacs tickling her nose. Mmm, lilacs. They even smelled purple; they brought back pleasant memories of her Grandma Belle. Yes, little Grandma Belle, who smelled like talcum powder and dressed in shades of violet.

"And feel this. It's from the park across the street. The blue jay's loss, but our gain," the clear voice tinkled.

Powder soft, a feather stroked across her forehead, dallied down her cheek, and gently swept under her chin. Meandering over folds in her neck and into nooks behind her earlobes, the downy quill discovered a new path and traced it up the other side of her face. Then, a playful swipe to her nose, like dotting an "i," and the feather was gone.

"Oh, and what would spring be without its sounds?"

Magically, the chirping of birds filled and flooded her room. The music was light and airy. The simple melody flowed from engaging to majestic and on to joyous. She could almost see the birds climbing and dipping and winging their way across the sky. Twittering, trilling, thrilling her with sweetness and filling her with the goodness of life.

A smile stole across Brenda's face, crinkling the corners of her closed eyes, tweaking the edges of her mouth, and sneaking onto her parted lips.

Brenda didn't see the new volunteer slip out of her room.

Brenda didn't hear the door whisper shut.

Brenda didn't feel alone.

The cassette player still warbled. The oxygen pulsed on.

DANIEL'S GIFT

*T*he antiseptic smell grew stronger as I hurried along the silent corridor. Ahead lay the isolation wing of the veteran's hospital. Every day for the past three months I had worn a path across the gray vinyl tiles. I was beginning to despair of this place and the reason that brought me here.

My brother, Eric, not only had a weak heart, but he had fallen and was now confined to bed with a fractured leg. Before he could recover from a bout of simple pneumonia, he had contracted a more virulent strain.

His doctor said he was failing and if he did not begin to walk he had no chance for recovery. He had to get up and start moving again.

For the past week Eric had moaned, "I'll never get out of this bed. My weak legs won't hold me up. I'm dying."

I explained that muscles take a long time before they atrophy, and he shouldn't give up. "A child learns to walk. You can again. It just takes time," I assured him.

Refusing to listen to the doctors, nurses, or me, Eric snapped, "Not after you've been in bed this long."

Now, my steps slowed at the door to his room. What would his mental outlook be today? I put on a mask. Sucked in a calming breath. Pushed open the door.

No hello. Just, "I want to die." That was his greeting for me, just as it had been his greeting yesterday and the day before.

Feeling I was losing the battle to change his attitude, I got a bit testy. My voice was louder than normal when I snapped, "Eric. You've got to believe you can get out of that bed."

He muttered, "Nah," and waved me off. Why had I even come? Eric kept telling me not to bother. But I couldn't abandon him. I was all he had.

I noticed he was staring toward the open door.

When I turned around, I saw a man in his sixties, wearing government-issue pajamas and a robe. His reddish-gray hair was curly, and he had the purest blue eyes I'd ever seen. He smiled broadly and walked into the room.

He went directly to Eric's bedside. "Remember me?" he asked with a soft French accent.

Eric shook his head.

The veteran squeezed Eric's hand. "You and I were in this hospital a couple years ago. Your name is Eric, and you're from New York, right?"

"That's right," Eric furrowed his brow. "But I don't remember you."

"I was in bed for almost two years. With physical therapy, I learned to walk again." The man stepped lightly to show how agile he was.

My brother's eyes widened as he studied his visitor. "How did you do that?"

"Therapy. Hard work—and painful sometimes. You just take it one day at a time."

"What's your name?" I asked, thinking that might jog Eric's memory.

"Daniel," the man replied.

He gave my brother a few pointers on gaining strength in his arms and legs, and told him how to ease himself out of bed and into a wheelchair. Then, on a napkin, he drew a happy face.

A cautious optimism shone in Eric's eyes.

Pleased that Eric had begun to rally from his funk, I listened as Daniel offered more words of comfort and other tips he had learned. Then he shook my hand, turned, and walked across the hall to his room.

"See?" I said. "He's older than you are. And if he can walk after being in bed for a long time, you should be able to do it, too."

Eric frowned, and I could tell he was thinking about what Daniel had said. For the first time in weeks, he gave me a sickly half-smile.

Within a few days, Eric had gotten himself out of bed and into a wheelchair. He began to grin and joke with me again.

He was more like the old Eric. Taped to the wall was the happy face napkin.

I wanted to thank Daniel and tell him that his words of comfort and encouragement had inspired my brother to get out of bed and get back on the path to recovery. However, I learned that he had already been discharged. I was sorry he wasn't there to see how much Eric was improving every day.

Slowly, Eric began to walk, and his health gradually improved. Each time I saw the smiley face taped to the wall, I remembered how Daniel had come through for my brother exactly when he needed it.

**The ignorant say that they will believe in angels only when they see them.
The wise understand that they will see angels only when they believe in them.**

HEALING A BROKEN HEART

*A*ngels appear to us in times of sorrow and grief to help us mend our broken hearts. After hearing my father's story, I am convinced of it.

I have many fond childhood memories and consider myself very lucky to have been raised by two special parents. Mom and Dad were totally devoted to one another; she was the love of his life. They raised their three daughters with warmth and humor, and they gave us a home filled with love and security.

My mother battled emphysema, and during the last two years of her life she was confined to a respirator. Dad was always there for her as she became more and more ill, and their roles gradually reversed. He did the shopping, cooking, and cleaning, caring for Mom as she had done for him for years. He never complained and seemed happy for the chance to care for his beloved wife. One night, she died peacefully in her sleep.

My sisters and I tried to comfort Dad as we all mourned together. He missed her terribly, the love of his life. As we sat together, Dad told us, "You know, I've never been alone. I went from home to college, into the Navy, then I married your mother. This is the first time I've been on my own." He was 73 years old.

The city my folks lived in had a music and crafts festival along the main street every year. My parents had always enjoyed this event—strolling the streets, enjoying the music, viewing the art displays, and delighting in the general air of friendliness and fun. Once again, the festival was scheduled, but Dad wondered if he'd enjoy it alone. He decided he needed to get out and mingle with people to combat his grief and take his mind away from the solitary life he was now experiencing.

The day of the festival, Dad walked up and down the crowded streets, enjoying the sights, sounds, and smells, but as the heat intensified he found himself getting a little weary. He began to look for a sidewalk café where he could sip some lemonade and catch his breath.

He heard a voice call out to him, "Excuse me, sir, would you like to sit down?" He turned to find a pretty young woman smiling and motioning to a chair next to hers.

He accepted her offer, and they began talking about the fair, the weather, and general things that strangers chat about.

As Dad and the young lady conversed, she asked if he was married. He smiled sadly and began reminiscing about Mother. His sorrow and sense of loss were apparent, and the woman listened attentively. As Dad relayed the story to me later, he remarked how surprised he was that "a pretty young thing would let an old codger bend her ear." Surely, he thought, she would have preferred to be doing something a bit more fun!

After they had chatted a while, his new friend smiled and reached into a shopping bag that was sitting by her feet. She presented my dad with a gift, saying, "I bought this for myself because I collect angels, but I'd be delighted if you would accept this. I believe it was intended for you." In her hands was a small porcelain angel, sitting and mending a broken heart.

As my dad recounted this story to me a few days later, we both realized that theirs had not been a chance meeting. An angel had entered Dad's world with a gift to help heal his broken heart.

Dad passed on not long after that encounter. He had played a round of golf (his "second love") and, as usual, topped it off with an afternoon nap. He passed away in his sleep, and his heart was finally mended as he rejoined my mother, the love of his life.

As for that angel with the broken heart . . . it's my most valued possession.

On gossamer wings they move

as gentle breezes on a warm summer's eve,

quietly reminding us

that we are always watched over,

always loved.

A TEDDY BEAR ANGEL

On a cold December day, my 10-year-old son, Lance, and I headed to the mall. I wanted to get my holiday shopping out of the way—in fact, I wished the holidays themselves would just end. Ever since my son Timothy had died at age 14, it had been hard for me to feel much joy, and Christmas only made it worse. Although I felt his absence every day, this time of year was especially depressing. I wished that I could somehow move past my grief, but so far that had proved impossible. The sights and smells and sounds of the season—all of it!—combined to make my memories almost more than I could bear.

As we walked through the mall, I steeled myself against the carols piping through the loudspeakers. I strode with my head lowered so I wouldn't see the booth where Santa sat, surrounded by his elves and a flock of happy families, all waiting patiently in line to have their photos taken. *It's not fair*, I wailed inside my head. *Not fair, not fair!*

Lance and I wandered into a clothing store and headed in separate directions. As I was flipping aimlessly through the scarves, I heard someone ask, "Can I help you?" I turned around and saw a young man smiling sweetly.

"Have you seen my friend Bob?" he asked, holding out a sweater-adorned teddy bear. "His friend Billy just found a home, but he's got lots of other friends, if you're interested in adopting one of them."

I chuckled, suddenly noticing that the bears were strategically placed throughout the store. The salesclerk walked on to show the bear to other customers, and I continued to browse through the racks.

When Lance and I had decided on our purchases, we headed up to the register. I was sold on the teddy bears, so I decided to buy one for myself. The salesclerk turned to the shelves behind her, filled with bears, and asked if I wanted one with a green or blue sweater. When I chose green, she snatched one from the mass and tossed it on the counter. But just before she rang the teddy bear up, another salesclerk shouted, "Wait!" She reached behind the counter and pulled out a bear that she had adopted as her own. "Take this one," she said, smiling. "I've been taking care of him, but he needs a good home." I smiled back as I nodded my approval. It seemed fitting and sweet, as if I really would be taking care of him for her. Lance and I gathered our bags and headed back out into the mall.

"What's the bear's name?" my son asked.

I reached into the shopping bag and pulled out the bear. I gasped when I saw his name: Timothy.

No, it can't be, I thought. Not the name of all my emotions. Not the name that's been attached to so many joys and sorrows.

I had to sit down.

As I wept, I came to a realization. I knew that no matter what, no matter when or where, my beloved son Timothy would always be with me, would always be in my heart. Tim hadn't disappeared into oblivion—he was up in heaven, watching and loving me, together with the Lord. Somehow, those thoughts made me feel better. I knew this wouldn't be the end of my pain—it would never go away completely. But for the first time in a long while, my heart seemed a little lighter and I actually felt a sense of joy.

I grabbed the teddy bear and my son and held them tight. Then I put the bear in the bag, wiped the tears from my eyes, and stood up. I was ready to move on.

To sense the presence of an angel
is like feeling the wind all around you.
You cannot actually see the wind, but you notice
its movement, and you know it is there.

A DAY OF HOPE

I drew in my raincoat against the chill as I followed my parents and my brother across the grounds of the Normandy American Military Cemetery in Colleville-sur-Mer, France.

What's wrong with me? I asked myself. This should have been a heart-pounding, momentous occasion for the whole family. Surely it was for Mom. For the first time in her life, she would stand at the grave of her father, Glen Edward Kuhn, a man she had never really known. He was killed in World War II on Mom's first birthday, July 29, 1944, and visiting his grave site was something she had always wanted to do. A good daughter would be right by her side, but standing there in an ocean of headstones I just wished I could wait in the car.

Seeing Omaha beach had been hard enough. It made me sick to my stomach to imagine those men—boys, really— storming out of the water that lapped so quietly at my feet. So many of them never left Normandy and are now laid out in military precision under that green lawn, marked by thousands of marble crosses and Stars of David. I read the names and dates on marker after marker and did quick calculations of the years from birth to death. Robert, William, John—those strangers who shared the names of some of my friends at school were my age, 19.

My stomach was tied up in knots, and I ached for those boys and for their families, too, because I knew my mother's loss. It would be hard enough to lose your father, but to have him taken on your birthday! Even though Grandma had eventually remarried, and Granddaddy Farley always loved Mom as one of his own, for her, birthdays must have always been tinged with a little sadness. After the cake had been eaten and the night had grown still, she must have thought of her father, wondering what his laughter sounded like, how he had walked across a room, and what he'd thought of his baby girl.

I was sad for my mom, but it wasn't just sadness I felt. My stomach hurt for my own guilt and frustration as well. Standing before those headstones, I could hear my own life's minutes ticking by. Each of those boys had made such a profound contribution to the world, laying down their lives for what they believed in. I, on the other hand, was lucky enough to have a whole future ahead of me, and yet I couldn't seem to choose any direction for my life. What contribution would I make?

My friends seemed to have their whole lives planned out. But me? My biochemistry degree was halfway done, and I still didn't know what I wanted to do with it—if anything. I knew that I wanted to serve God in some way, but how? My future plans reached only as far as the end of the summer. The moment we got home from France, I'd be repacking the car and heading out for a summer job as a youth minister in rural North Carolina. Would the ministry be my calling? What about teaching? If only God would make it clear how he wished me to serve!

As we walked to the visitors' center, Mom talked nervously and fingered the bouquet of flowers we'd brought for her father's grave. Inside the center, a young woman behind the desk welcomed us with a warm smile. She couldn't have been much older than I was. Her long, brown hair was pulled back into a ponytail, and her eyes were kind and sincere. Her English lilted with a French accent as she greeted us and then asked, "And what is the soldier's name?"

"Glen Edward Kuhn," my mother answered. "My father died on July 29, 1944." I could hear the slight tremble in her voice.

The woman looked through her book to find his name and then pointed on a map. "His grave is here," she said. "I would be honored to take you there." At our nod, she picked up a pail and a cloth from behind the desk, and Mom followed her, then my father and my brother and, finally, me. The wind whipped our raincoats around. A quiet rain began as we turned down his row, searching the headstones for his name.

Our guide stopped, and we all fixed our eyes on the name on the cross. We read and reread the words:

GLEN E. KUHN
S SGT 83 QM CO 83 DIV
TENNESSEE JULY 29, 1944

After a quiet moment, our guide set her pail and cloth next to the cross. Gathering her skirt to one side, she knelt in front of the cross, pressing her bare knees into the wet grass. As the wind blew her hair about, she scooped up clumps of wet sand and rubbed them into the grooves of the carved lettering with her fingers, as gently as if she was putting ointment on a wound. She moved with quiet reverence, but what was she doing? It just seemed to make a dirty mess on the cross.

I looked to Dad for explanation. He stood close to Mom, watching. No one spoke.

When every groove was covered, she picked up the clean cotton cloth and rubbed it over the cross, slowly, gingerly brushing off the scattered sand. The wet sand left in the lettering was like dark brown paint on the freshly polished cross. In an ocean of white gravestones, my grandfather's name stood out from them all.

As we drew closer to examine her work, our guide gathered her things and then shook each of our hands, thanking us for his sacrifice. I wish I could remember her words, because they were sincere and kind, but over the years they've slipped away. What remains in my memory, as clearly as if it had happened only a moment ago, is the reverential way in which she knelt down in front of that cross to serve my mother and my family. She was no pastor or missionary, but she surely ministered to us. As she filled in the letters on that cross, God was writing his own words on my heart:

"This is how to serve me. Do all that you do with respect and humility and love, as if you were doing it for me."

The day after we returned from France, I began my summer of youth ministry. Although I loved the kids, the Bible studies, and even the car washes and bowling marathons, it was not the end of my career search. In fact, I'm still searching. I've enjoyed plenty of work opportunities—as a chemist in a lab, a high school chemistry teacher, a volunteer, and a mom. I've tried to follow that young French woman's example of humble service in whatever job I'm doing.

Along my winding route, God has sprinkled in a few surprises. Though I never imagined I'd go back to France, my husband and I ended up moving there, to the little village of Aubiére, just a day's drive away from the Normandy cemetery and beaches. And July 29, which had always been a special day on my calendar, is now circled for yet another reason. Eight years after touring that cemetery, on July 29, 1992, my mom received an extra-special birthday gift. Her first grandson, my son Benjamin, arrived. So a day that was once tinged with sadness has now been blessed with hope. It illustrates to me once again that I needn't worry about the details of my life—as long as I'm willing to follow God, he'll lead me where I need to go.

In the most unlikely of places—waiting in your shadow, perhaps—the most improbable of angels waits for you.

LOOK FOR THE SILVER LINING

I was having an especially stressful week. My family, my job, even the other people at church were pushing my nerves to the breaking point. I was getting ready to scream or cry, and I wasn't sure which it would be.

I was standing in my kitchen having my morning cup of coffee, when suddenly, from out of nowhere, I heard music. I thought, *Why is the ice cream truck coming so early in the morning?* And then I realized the sound was coming from the top of my piano, where my music box collection was displayed. I raced into the living room and was amazed to see my mother's golden angel slowly waltzing around the top of the music box. The melody "Look for the Silver Lining" rang joyously in my ears.

I couldn't imagine who—or what—had turned the music box on. No train had rumbled by, no jets had passed overhead, no hand had touched the music box.

My mother had passed away ten years before, but I knew she was still reaching out to me in some miraculous way, encouraging me to have a positive attitude in my life. As I listened to the lovely melody streaming from that little music box, I felt her presence all around me.

The mechanism on my mother's music box, now *my* music box, had worn out ages ago, and it hadn't worked for several years. But that music box sprang back to life that day—at the exact time that I needed it most—lifting my spirits, completely changing my attitude, and reminding me to look for the best in whatever I encounter... encouraging me, indeed, to "look for the silver lining."

How grateful I am for that revitalizing melody. I have no doubt that my mother's spirit sent me those notes of joy.

Since that day, I have tried again and again to get the angel to play its sweet music, but to no avail. I guess if I really need to hear that song again, an angel will intervene.

In a moment of quiet, dark stillness, or even in
the bustle of daily life,
you may occasionally feel that you are in the
company of an angel.
Revel in its divine presence!

FLYING IN FORMATION

Suzanne rested her back against the airplane seat. She was exhausted! The last few days had been the hardest of her life.

Her father's death was so unexpected. Sixty-two was too young to die. He'd always said he'd never get old, but everybody knew that he really meant he didn't want to end up needing other people to care for him. Not that anyone would have minded.

"Hoot," as everyone called him, was a hoot. He always had a smile, a joke to tell, a trick to play. But it hadn't been his sense of humor that had earned him the nickname. He'd been a wildlife carver who had created wonderfully realistic renditions of birds and waterfowl. How lucky they were to have his carvings as a tangible legacy. Every time she saw the Canada goose in her entryway, Suzanne would be reminded of him.

When they were growing up, she and Jake and Micah had spent hours in their dad's studio. They battled wood dust when they came in for help with their homework and endured the smell of turpentine when they came in to bargain for a later curfew. They learned life's lessons amid the ducks and songbirds their dad had spent so much of his free time carving out of wood.

He always used bird analogies to explain things. They practiced turning their heads like owls so they would remember to look at problems from all directions. He explained how duck hunters used decoys while warning the kids not to be fooled by friends who said drugs wouldn't hurt them. When he was alive, Hoot had hated to hear his children arguing. He always encouraged them to work together. "Family is forever," he'd say. He reminded them of the Canada geese that flew over their summer place in Michigan. "See," he'd say, "how they move in formation. Moving that way makes it easier for all of them to fly."

Suzanne looked out the airplane window. Her eyes misted over as she thought back to the night she was told of her dad's death. At least he died in his sleep. But none of them had been there.

She and Jake and Micah had flown to Chicago as soon as they heard. The first morning they huddled, heartbroken, around the kitchen table. Jake had searched Hoot's files for any papers that might help them make final arrangements. He found duck patterns and the entry form for the National Carver's Show in Ocean City, Maryland, but no will and nothing about his father's wishes.

"It's obvious that Dad hadn't planned on dying anytime soon," said Jake. There were unpaid bills stuffed in the spice rack, and they couldn't even locate his checkbook.

"First things first," said Micah. "We've got to make the funeral arrangements."

They moved out to the deck with their coffee and the bagels the neighbors had brought by. Edgy from lack of sleep and overwhelmed by their loss, they began to argue.

Suzanne had been sure Hoot would have wanted to be cremated.

"No way," said Jake.

The argument intensified. "Fine," Suzanne said. "Do it your way. I'll just let you two make all the decisions." As she flounced off, they heard a strange honking sound overhead.

They looked up. A flock of Canada geese in perfect formation was circling above the house.

They stared at each other in amazement. Canada geese didn't head down from the upper peninsula until much later in the summer.

They hadn't had to translate the honks. They'd gotten the message. Together they made the rest of the decisions without further disagreement.

Suzanne smiled and closed her eyes as the plane soared homeward.

The guardian angels of life sometimes fly so high as to be beyond our sight, but they are always looking down upon us.

—JEAN PAUL RICHTER

FAITHFUL ANGELS

Twists and turns, corners we cannot negotiate. This is the nature of an angel's world: helping us with the unknown challenges as well as the ones that stare us in the face.

❦❦❦

THE EYES OF AN ENEMY

The first time I saw my compassionate enemy, he was pointing a machine gun at us. It was early spring of 1945, and my grandparents and I had just emerged from a bunker where we had spent a terror-filled night.

I was nine years old then, living in Hungary, completely surrounded by World War II. War was almost all I had known during my nine years; it seemed as though no place was safe. My grandparents, who were raising me, and I had been on the road in our horse-drawn wagon for many months, searching for a safe place to live. We left our village in the Bacska region because Marshal Tito and his Communist partisans were closing in on it. Grandfather decided that a rural area would be safer. So we moved to one in upper Hungary and settled in a small house next to an old cemetery. Here, Grandfather, with the help of some distant neighbors, built a bunker in a flat area behind the house. And on that early spring day in 1945, we spent the entire night in the bunker.

Warplanes droned, tanks thundered, and bombs exploded over our heads all night, but at dawn everything grew deathly still. Grandfather decided that it would be safe to go back to our house. Cautiously we crept out into the light of early day and headed toward the house. The brush crackled under our feet as we walked past the cemetery. The markers looked lonely, separated by tall, dry weeds. I shivered, holding tightly to my orange tabby cat.

Suddenly, there was a rustle in the bushes just ahead. Two men jumped out and pointed machine guns directly at us.

"Stoi!" one of the men shouted. Since we were from an area where both Serbian and Hungarian was spoken, we knew the word meant, "Stop!"

"Russians!" Grandfather whispered in alarm. "Stand very still, and keep quiet."

But I was already running after my cat. She had leapt out of my arms when the soldier shouted, so I darted between the soldiers and scooped her up. The younger of the two soldiers approached me. I cringed, holding Paprika against my chest. The soldier reached out and petted her.

"I have a little girl about your age back in Russia, and she has a cat just like this one," he said. He gently tugged one of my blond braids. "And she has long braids, too, just like you." I looked up into a pair of kind brown eyes, and my fear vanished. Together, Grandfather and Grandmother sighed in relief.

Both soldiers came back to the house with us and shared in our meager breakfast, and we found out from them that the Soviet occupation of Hungary was in progress.

In the following months, many atrocities took place throughout our country, our area included, but because the young Russian soldier had taken a liking to me, we were spared from the worst of it. Ivan came to visit often, bringing little treats for Paprika and me, and he always talked longingly of his own little girl. I loved his visits, yet I was terrified of the Russians in general. Then one day, almost a year later, he had some news.

"I've been transferred to another area, malka (little one), so I won't be able to come and visit anymore. But I have a gift for you," he said, taking something out of his pocket. It was a necklace with a turquoise Russian Orthodox cross on it. It was the most beautiful thing I had even seen, let alone owned. He placed it around my neck. "You wear this at all times, malka. God will protect you from harm." I hugged him tight and then sadly watched him drive away.

World War II was over, but the people of Hungary still felt the repercussions. Many men who had been involved in politics or deemed undesirable were rounded up by the secret police, never to be seen again. My own grandfather was taken away, but he managed to escape and go into hiding. Miraculously, my grandmother and I were reunited with him in 1947. We had gotten counterfeit papers so we could cross the Austrian border in a transport truck filled with ethnic Germans from Hungary. It was there that we met up with Grandfather.

Along with dozens of other people, the three of us boarded the transport truck, fake papers in hand. I knew if we were found out, Grandpa would be hauled off to prison and might even be executed. I glanced toward the Russian soldiers who were coming closer to inspect the papers, and I prayed to God to keep us safe.

I looked up as a guard boarded the truck. I caught my breath. "Grandpa," I whispered. "Look, it's my soldier, Ivan! He is checking this truck!"

I wanted to leap up and run to him, but Grandpa shushed me cautiously. "Maybe he won't recognize us," he whispered, pulling his knit hat further down his forehead. Grandpa was afraid of Ivan now.

Then he was before us. My grandfather handed over our papers without looking up. I leaned closer and put my hand protectively on his shoulder while I peered cautiously at Ivan, hoping to see the old, kind sparkle in his eyes. But he was intent upon the papers, his expression grave. I didn't dare to breathe. At last he handed the papers back to Grandpa.

"Everything is in order in this vehicle," he finally said. Then, winking at me, he got down off the vehicle, and in an instant the truck began to move. I looked over my shoulder and caught his eye. "Thank you," I mouthed the words, holding up the cross that hung around my neck. He nodded discreetly, then quickly turned and walked away. As we crossed the border to safety, we all sighed in relief and said a prayer of thanks to the Lord.

Although we suffered greatly during the war, the memory of one blessing will always stay with me: the kind soldier who turned my fear to faith and showed me that God's compassion can be found anywhere, even in the eyes of an enemy.

Fear not, for a mighty shield of love protects you.
Doubt not, for mighty wings of faith surround you.

PASS IT ON

*R*uth Cardin came into my life when I was 25 and she was 47. We worked together for nine months. Then I didn't see her for nearly 40 years. Yet her one act of compassion reverberated throughout my life.

I took a teaching job at Nevada Union High School in the beautiful mountain town of Grass Valley, California. Ruth was the school's English Department head. Although we had a cordial relationship as colleagues, we didn't know each other well outside of school.

In August I rented a cottage for my four-year-old daughter and myself. My husband, Ed, attended Stanford University 200 miles away in Palo Alto, so we had a "weekend" marriage during the 1960–61 school year. He had a scholarship and worked in the cafeteria to make living expenses. As a teacher, I made very little money. From my net pay of $225 a month, I paid $50 for rent, $50 for babysitting, and $50 for food. The other $75 had to cover gas, auto maintenance, utilities, clothes, and entertainment. Obviously, money was quite tight.

One Sunday in January, Ed was with me when I doubled over with severe stomach pains.

The pain was unbearable. Ed drove us to the emergency room at Sierra Nevada Hospital. Appendicitis was the diagnosis. That meant an operation and two weeks of recuperation. I had medical coverage but very few sick days.

"This is awful," I told Ed as we filled out countless forms. "I don't know many people here. Will you call the babysitter and see if she can take Sherri for two weeks? And please call the school, too."

Ed did. He also called Ruth Cardin. Then, after the operation, he headed back to Stanford.

Once the physical pain had abated, I lay in my hospital bed and fretted about finances. I'd need extra money for the sitter, and I'd also need money for medicine.

Ruth appeared in my room four days after the operation. She assured me that the substitute teacher was competent but the students missed me and sent their best wishes. Then she handed me a check for $50.

"I know that illnesses can be expensive," she said. "I don't want you to repay me. This is a gift. When you can, give money to someone else who needs it."

I was flabbergasted. No one, friend or relative, had ever voluntarily offered me money. I thanked her effusively, a bit dazed that she would offer unsolicited help when I most needed it. Remember, in 1961, $50 was a lot of money.

Ruth and I became very friendly during the next months. I truly hated to leave Grass Valley and my teaching position, but Ed had graduated and landed a job in San Francisco.

For the next few years Ruth and I corresponded but didn't see each other. I had another child, and Ed changed jobs frequently. Somehow, despite my efforts, I could never accumulate an extra $50 that I could give away.

Finally, ten years later, I helped one of my students. He needed $70 for a bus trip to visit his father in Texas. I told Robert the same thing Ruth had told me: "Pass this money to someone else who needs it."

Robert wrote five years later to say that he'd given $100 to a friend who couldn't pay his utility bill. I'm hoping that the chain connecting all of us has lengthened and touched many other people.

When I moved back to Grass Valley in 1998, I found Ruth's phone number and called. She was glad to hear from me, and I was happy to reconnect with such a special lady. At 87, her health was failing, but her wit and her faith were as sharp as ever.

Who knows how many lives have been affected by Ruth Cardin's initial gift? I know that she affected me profoundly. Maybe we can't alter the world for better in a noticeable way, but we can alter our little corner. Ruth certainly did that for me.

To live as the angels do, give more than you receive,
and love more than you are loved.

IN MEMORY OF LIBERTY

My daughter, Liberty, was born with a hole in her heart. When she finally came home from the hospital, my wife and I kept her close to us at all times. She slept quietly, and we took turns resting the tips of our fingers on her chest, counting her tiny heartbeats. My wife and I did not talk much those days. We looked at each other and our precious daughter, we cried, we prayed, and we counted.

Sadly, there was no miracle to speak of. Liberty, so small and so tired, managed to give us a tiny smile just seconds before God took her to heaven, where she could finally rest. She would be my only child. And still, 17 years later, I miss her tremendously.

After Liberty's death, my wife and I grew further and further apart until we finally couldn't remember a time when we had felt close to each other. It wasn't a difficult divorce. Looking back now, I realize we should have cried more.

I began to move often. I followed jobs, weather, whims, and sometimes women to far states and distant countries. Each time I arrived in one place, I began to search for reasons to leave. I worked many different jobs—too many jobs to ever excel at any of them. I didn't feel like I was searching; I felt like I was running.

As the years passed, my life grew steadily more chaotic. I'd have months of quiet and then somehow I would sabotage things and send myself reeling into a new city, penniless, paranoid, and aching to rest. I contemplated suicide, but I believed in God too strongly. Even though I was exhausted and miserable, I knew that eventually, with faith, I would find my way.

Finally, one miserable winter after years of destructive living, I once again found myself with no place to live. I had just arrived in Chicago in search of a distant friend who I thought could help me out. I hadn't worked in months, and the money I'd managed to save, I kept with me. On the bus from Minnesota, someone stole my wallet, and I was left with just enough money for a local phone call. But there was no one for me to call. I wandered around the big city, thinking about my options. Should I go to a shelter? Could I sleep in a park? Should I find a church?

I was afraid I might freeze to death looking for somewhere to stay. I walked and walked, keeping my head down against the slicing wind. The sting of the bitter air was so cold, it felt curiously hot.

I glanced in the window of a coffeehouse. I didn't have enough money for a cup of coffee, but I couldn't keep myself from going in. People were sitting comfortably, drinking from their big mugs, reading newspapers, talking with friends. It was so warm inside that the young woman playing guitar was wearing a T-shirt. I figured I'd go in and stare at the artwork on the walls or look at the newspapers to buy myself some time away from the cold.

There were lots of young people inside, relaxing and enjoying themselves. They seemed like they had the luxury of not being burdened with worries. They seemed like the kind of people who had good jobs, loving partners, and children who don't die of holes in the heart.

The young woman tuning her guitar was a different story. She looked nervous. She was sweating, but it wasn't that warm. I found a small corner table away from the manager's view and borrowed a cup from a vacated table so I'd look like a customer, too.

The young woman was still tuning her guitar. Although she was looking down at the strings and her fingers, her eyes were open wide. She looked as though she was trying to keep from crying.

Next to me, two men were playing chess, deep in concentration. A dozen laughing people were having a wonderful time at a table right in front of the guitar player. I looked around. No one else knew that just like me, the young woman wanted to be somewhere else. Somewhere, perhaps, where she felt more comfortable.

Eventually she began to sing. She still didn't look up, and her eyes stayed wide open. She sang the first song so faintly, I couldn't hear a single word. Nobody else in the whole joint seemed to notice her.

I watched her closely. She paused for a moment, and I realized she had finished her first song. I clapped. I might have been the only one who clapped at first, but I did it so loudly, it seemed to remind everyone else of the woman's existence, so they halfheartedly clapped as well. She smiled, still looking down.

The next song ended with another tentative pause. I clapped loudly again, and—after a bit of hesitation and looking around—the others clapped, too. Truthfully, we still couldn't hear her, but we all clapped politely. This time she looked up for a split second; the expression on her face wasn't pleasure, but relief.

I could hear the next song. It was about love. She sang it softly, but I could make out almost every word. I liked her voice. It had a texture I didn't expect it to have. It was low, yet sweet. To this day, I can't really explain why I enjoyed listening to her so much.

I paid close attention and clapped after every song. Each time we clapped, she glanced up or smiled, and each time she would sing a little louder. The louder she got, the happier I became.

During her break, she tuned her guitar and studied her notes, and the manager came around with a basket for tips. My heart sank. She was the age my daughter would have been, she was nervous, and she made me so happy I didn't care about not having a place to sleep. I wanted to give her something. Yet I had nothing.

I borrowed a pen and paper from another customer, and as she tuned her guitar, I wrote to her about my daughter, about the cold, and about how happy I was—how privileged—to have heard her sing. I apologized for not having the money to show her my appreciation, but I told her that if my pockets were filled with gold coins right now, I would toss them all in her basket and consider hearing her sing worth every last bit of riches. I told her I would pray for her—pray that she would find the courage to share her voice with the world and to be proud and strong.

The basket kept circulating, and the coins were clanking as she began to sing again. This time she kept her chin up and looked out into the room. She sang and smiled, and I clapped my hands like a thousand hearts beating.

I could have stayed for hours, but I decided to face the looming night ahead of me. I walked around as much as I could bear to, and then I borrowed some change and ended up riding the train back and forth, north and south into the night.

The next evening, I went back to the coffeehouse to see if the young woman was singing again. I looked through the large, slowly fogging windows. I couldn't see her.

But I did see the manager waving his arms at me. Me? I motioned, pointing to my chest.

The manager nodded excitedly. "Come in, come in," I could see him saying as he pushed chairs aside to get to the door.

He didn't look angry, but I couldn't be sure. I thought about running. "Sir? Did I do something?"

The manager put his hands on my shoulders. "Well, yes! Yes, you did something."

"I don't understand. I didn't do anything. . . ."

"You clapped for my daughter. You made her so happy. I want to thank you, my friend."

"Your daughter?" I couldn't believe it.

The manager laughed. "Come in from the cold. Have a cup of coffee with me."

"Sir, thank you. The truth is, I don't have money for coffee tonight."

Refusing to take no for an answer, the manager drew me in. We sat down at the table in front of the fireplace, and, after settling me in place and making sure I was comfortable, he brought over muffins and coffee, then a giant bowl of soup. We discussed his shy daughter and how courageous she now felt. As soon as she had read my note, she knew exactly who I was. We talked about the cold and about babies who die even though you count their heartbeats. We talked about strange cities and happier times.

Eric, the manager and now my friend, offered me a generous amount of cash to help me out. I wouldn't accept it. Then he leaned in close and spoke with a kindness I had forgotten existed in this world. He told me I should consider it a loan.

"A loan?"

"That's right, a loan. You can pay me $20 a week from your paycheck. That is, of course, if you want a job."

There were no papers, no references, no fear. I had no address, no telephone. We made that deal on a handshake and on faith. I felt like the richest man alive.

Life is steady now. I'm still in Chicago, and I still clap loudly at the coffeehouse where Eric and I became friends and eventually business partners. Lauren, Eric's daughter, now sings in a theater in town. She is poised and lovely, and when she sings, her eyes and smile light up the room.

Some people search all their lives for glimpses of angels. I have been lucky. I held one angel in my arms and counted her heartbeats; to another angel, I gave a standing ovation. God has shown me that it is possible to fill the holes in our hearts.

What know we of the Blest above
But that they sing, and that they love?

—WILLIAM WORDSWORTH

ALARM BELLS

*F*all had settled over the community in a blaze of glory: maples, oaks with their purplish-brown leaves, hawthorns with red berries clumped at the end of the branches.

It may have been the dry summer or the dusty, dry fall now underway that unleashed all the germs early, but it was the worst flu season in memory. Newscasters were predicting one of the worst winters for illnesses.

It hit Sara the week before Halloween.

She was sidelined for two days with a headache, cough, and fever. Finally she went to the doctor, who, while he sympathized, was himself sneezing up a storm. He sent her home with pills and potions that "knocked her out," as she put it.

"At least while you're sleeping, you won't be coughing," said her husband sympathetically, pulling on his work gloves and hunting for the matches. "You rest," he advised. There was very little wind that day, and he was going out to rake and burn the leaves while she slept. "When I come in, I'll fix you a nice supper," he promised.

Sara smiled to herself as she lay down on the couch, pulling the quilt up to her chin. Her husband's idea of fixing a nice supper was opening a can of soup, heating the contents, and serving it on a tray with crackers arranged around the soup bowl like sunflower petals! But at least he was thoughtful and caring. That's what gave the soup he offered that special taste, that little extra something.

For 35 years he had been doing just such thoughtful things. She was a fortunate lady, if you believed half the tales you saw on TV or read in magazines. Or, she had to admit sadly, even if she listened to some of her friends.

Succumbing to the medicine's pull, she drifted off into a deep, drug-induced slumber with a smile on her face thinking of this special man puttering in the backyard with his rake and wagon. He loved being busy. Retirement had not slowed him down a bit; it just gave him more time to think up projects to accomplish.

Sara was sound asleep when someone started pounding on her back door. Groggily, she got to her feet. "I'm coming," she called, pulling on her bathrobe. In her confused haste, Sara tripped over the quilt. She gathered it in her arms to avoid falling.

"Hurry!" shouted the person at the door.

When she opened it, however, there was no one there . . . only her husband out by the road burning leaves in the ditch. As she watched, he somehow lost his balance and fell into the flames.

He couldn't get up.

It was as if Sara's bathrobe had wings. She got to the fire in time to pull him to safety and wrap him in the quilt she had been dragging.

"No," he told her later at the hospital, "I didn't see anybody in the yard or on the porch coming to get you. It was just my lucky day that you woke up when you did."

They held hands until the nurse brought him his supper: soup that Sara fed him, after she blessed it with a prayer for its nourishment and with a thank-you to the angel who had given her more time with her husband here on Earth.

An angel doesn't have to speak to be heard,
be visible to be seen, or be present to be felt.
Believe in angels, and they will always be near.

I HEAR YOU

*W*alking through the drugstore, I noticed the young salesclerk.

Her name tag read "Darla," and I recognized her as the little girl I used to babysit many years before. I watched as she wrote a note to a customer. Darla had been born deaf, and this simple method (despite hours of signing and speaking training) seemed to be her preferred method of communicating with the public.

It must have been well over 20 years since "the event" had taken place. I thought of what could have been, of the tragedy that would have touched so many lives if things had turned out just slightly different.

At the hopeful age of 14, I had a thriving babysitting business. I was watching Darla and Billy during the summer months while their parents went to work. Darla had just had a birthday, and she'd gotten her first bike, a metallic blue number with high handlebars and a banana seat. Darla thought she was the coolest thing on two wheels (or four, to be precise, since she still needed training wheels), and I loved watching the joy on her pretty face as she rode her new gift.

Darla's father had insisted that she ride the bike in the driveway unless he was with her. As he signed this to her, she moaned and turned away—the typical response when she didn't want to "see" what you were saying.

"I'll watch her," I promised. "I won't let her out in the street."

He looked worried, but he nodded his approval and left for work, waving good-bye to the kids and me.

Darla's brother, Billy, who was jealous of all the attention his sister was getting, was in the yard doing somersaults and cartwheels, desperately trying to draw me to him. Darla rode her bike in the large driveway, circling proudly, waving each time she passed.

Then I heard the squealing tires of a car speeding into the subdivision. They say that a plane crash occurs when more than one probable calamity occurs at the same time. In a similar vein, our small world seemed about to crash.

First, Billy fell doing a cartwheel and hit his head on a brick. He started crying, and the small trickle of blood that ran down the side of his face sent him into hysterics. Darla, unable to hear the sound of her brother crying or the car speeding in our direction, decided at that moment to try out her new bike in the street. Too far away to stop her, I could only watch, my heart pounding so hard it hurt, as she sped out of the driveway. The car was coming closer and closer, and I was powerless to do anything.

Scooping Billy up, I ran after Darla, but I didn't stand a chance—she had too much of a lead on me. As soon as I saw the car, its driver also saw Darla, who was now in the middle of the street, pedaling and looking up at a small flock of starlings flying overhead. The driver honked and yelled at her, but he did not slow down. In an instant Darla was going to be hit.

"She's deaf! Stop!" I screamed at the car, but the radio was so loud that the driver couldn't hear me. I felt a swoosh of cold air as the car flew past me.

I screamed at Darla to stop, then I shielded Billy's eyes from what I knew was going to be a horrible scene.

The driver finally realized that Darla was not going to move in time, so he tried to stop. His brakes screeched, and his front end started to turn as he began sliding sideways down the pavement. The tires smoked, but he couldn't stop the heavy vehicle at that speed.

At just that moment, one bird from the flock of starlings swooped down in front of Darla and landed in a tree by the side of the road. Darla followed its flight and turned her bike, pedaling to the tree for a closer look. The car, now almost fully sideways, slid behind her, barely missing the back of her bike. Darla stared happily at the bird, never seeing the car that had almost taken her life. The driver swore at her and sped away. But at least she was safe.

That moment, at the impressionable age of 14, I began to believe in God and angels. For years I thought about that tiny bird and why it flew to the tree at that exact moment, leaving its fellow travelers to fly on. It confirmed that even the smallest of things can change your life.

A tear ran down my cheek as I stood in the bright, orderly drugstore, thinking about all the tiny yet profound cross-roads in our lives—many of which we're not even aware. How thankful I was that God sent a angel in the form of a starling to save that little girl's life. I could only imagine what other miracles I'd never even noticed! Surely he puts us where we need to be exactly when we need to be there.

Darla finished helping another customer, and I walked over to say hello.

I have never seen my guardian angel, but I have felt her presence in times of duress, like a warm, comforting breath upon my face in a cold winter storm.

$\mathcal{F}$IGHTING $\mathcal{F}$ROM THE $\mathcal{H}$EART

$\mathcal{A}$nxiety mounted as the plane neared my destination of Eersol, Holland. It was 1984, and I was flying back to Holland with my son, Joseph, Jr., for a reunion with the man who had saved my life.

My mind flashed back to September 17, 1944, to another flight over Holland. It was the greatest airborne military operation in history: the invasion of Holland, the battle of Arnhem. About 35,000 Allied paratroopers were dropped behind Nazi lines in Holland to liberate that occupied country. At the same time, British ground forces would advance from Belgium.

But the Allies underestimated the strength of the German forces. By the time the British Army arrived—five days late—thousands of Allied troops had already been killed, captured, or wounded.

Our C-47 carried 18 paratroopers of the 101st Airborne and a crew of four: Guidio Brassesco, pilot; Joseph Andrews, copilot; Harry Tinckom, radio operator; and yours truly, Joseph Curreri, crew chief. As we flew toward our drop, an enemy antiaircraft shell exploded right in the middle of the plane's fuselage. In seconds the aircraft was blazing. Panicked paratroopers brushed by me and jumped, only to have trailing flames consume their chutes. I'd never jumped before, but I knew I had to bail out. With a prayer, I dove through a sheet of fire.

Landing in an open turnip field, I ran for cover in the nearby woods. Alone and unarmed, I was helpless and frightened. I wanted to reconnect with my crew, but I knew it would be perilous trying to make it through the unfamiliar woods, where I was certain to encounter enemy fire.

Suddenly a young Dutch civilian came from nowhere and shouted, "American? Vien avec moi." According to my rusty high school French, I understood him to say, "Follow me." Was he friend or foe? I had no way of knowing. I just had to trust him.

He could have been shot by the Nazis for helping an enemy soldier, but Adrian Goosens risked the consequences and hid me in his home. Then Nazi soldiers began searching houses for downed airmen, so Adrian hid me in the woods. There I was reunited with my crew members, and I was stunned to see all of them alive. Brassesco and Andrews had gone down with the plane and miraculously survived with broken bones, cuts, and burns. Members of the Dutch Underground had dragged them out of the burning aircraft. Tinckom, like me, had bailed out.

In the following days, diminutive, wiry Adrian scouted the area and warned our crew whenever the enemy was near. At one time, about 30 retreating Germans came within 20 yards of our hiding place and built a machine-gun nest. But thanks to Adrian's warning we had already dug foxholes. The two wounded pilots hid in one, and Harry and I hid in the other. We camouflaged both foxholes with brush and branches. After hiding (and praying) in tense silence for three hours, we saw the Nazis move on.

For five anxious days and sleepless nights, we hid in the woods waiting for the advancing British Army. Adrian and a nearby farmer fed us each night. I marveled at the courage of the Underground fighters, who included the local priest among their troops.

Finally the British arrived, and Adrian led them to our hiding place. We were rescued at last! I embraced Goosens and thanked him for everything he had done. He had saved our lives.

After the war, I returned home to my beloved family in Philadelphia and began a business career. But I never forgot the heroic deeds of the Dutch Underground, and especially of Adrian Goosens. How could I ever repay him?

In 1953, a devastating flood hit Holland. People were in dire need of food, clothing, and medicine. Reacting swiftly, I posted a sign in my shop's window: "We will collect any old clothing, shoes, and blankets for Holland's Flood Relief. The Dutch Underground helped us during the war. It's our turn now."

People responded overwhelmingly. I collected two truck-loads of clothing, shoes, and blankets and sent it through the Dutch Consulate to Holland.

Over the years I exchanged letters with Adrian, interpreted by his sister who understood English, and sent gifts. We both married, were each blessed with two children, suffered heart attacks, recovered, and retired.

As the years passed, the one great desire in my life was to meet, face to face, one more time the man who had saved my life. One day in 1984, I received a phone call: "This is Adrian Goosens from Holland!"

I almost dropped the phone. "Adrian?" I gasped. "It can't be!" He had learned to speak English, and he invited me to come and visit him for ten days. He told me, "Two airline tickets are on the way." Overwhelmed, tears rushed down my face.

As I prepared for my trip, I felt the urge to do something special for my friend. I shared my story with the mayor, who drew up an official greeting to Adrian and his comrades thanking them for their courage and heroics "in saving American lives during the war years."

The White House also responded to my plea with a beautiful color portrait of the President with the words, "To Adrian Goosens, with thanks and greetings from the American people." It was signed by Ronald Reagan.

When I arrived in Holland, Adrian Goosens met me at the gate. We embraced, and our tears flowed freely.

For ten unforgettable days, we remembered and retraced our dreadful days in the woods 40 years earlier. Amazingly, the foxholes we had dug were still there. Adrian introduced me to the beauty of the land and the warmth of the Dutch people. When I gave him the gifts I'd brought, he stammered and said, "It was my duty."

Adrian Goosens is now in heaven, but I'll always remember him and all those brave war heroes who risked their lives to save ours. Adrian may have felt he was just doing his duty, but I think what they did went above and beyond what they were expected to do. Those men weren't just acting out of duty. They were fighting from the heart.

Are not all angels ministering spirits sent to serve
those who will inherit salvation?

—HEBREWS 1:14

SWEET SURRENDER

Shortly after purchasing a beautiful oak dining room table and chairs, my husband and I discovered that our active family needed something more practical. Late Friday afternoon, I made arrangements to place an ad in the newspaper so we could sell our set and purchase one better suited to our needs. We confidently expected the phone to begin ringing on Monday morning.

While waiting for services to start on Sunday morning, I scanned the church bulletin. I immediately noticed an entry for a Russian ministry in need of household furniture. *I have a new dining room set I can give them,* I thought. I quickly pushed the thought out of my mind, reminding myself that we needed the money from the sale of our set in order to buy another set. We can't afford to just give the oak set away.

I told my husband about the notice in the bulletin and my subsequent thoughts, and Tom let me know that he supported either giving or selling the furniture. The decision was mine to make.

I wrestled in my spirit for the remainder of the day. I was unable to sleep that night as well. The notice stuck in my mind as a spiritual battle raged in my heart. Desperate to find peace, I sought middle ground. What if I donate the set if it doesn't sell within one week, I wondered. The suggestion of compromise made me feel even worse.

My spiritual fog gradually lifted as the choice became clear. When morning dawned, I gave in. Still in my bathrobe, I shuffled through the cluttered papers on the countertop, looking for the church bulletin. Like a child anxiously waiting to tell a big secret, now that I had made my decision I could hardly wait to make the call.

"Does your ministry need a dining room set?" I asked the woman who answered the phone.

Without hesitation, she effusively took me up on my offer. Compassion stirred in my heart as she told me about a Russian family of nine who had arrived in the United States with nothing but the clothes on their backs. "They have no furniture. Not even a table to eat on. They are a kind and generous family, and we know they would appreciate your gift." My heart swelled as I heard the story, and I was even more convinced that I had made the right decision.

After making arrangements to pick up the furniture, we were just about the hang up when she added, "Thank you for following your heart."

I wondered how she knew. I had not shared my story with her, as I was too ashamed to expose my spiritual struggle.

The Russian man arrived at our home with an interpreter later that day. His eyes watered when I led him to his new furniture. Although I didn't recognize his words, the emotion behind them was readily apparent. He wiped his wet cheeks. "He says he has never received anything so nice; he has never owned anything so nice. He is thankful," the interpreter explained.

"Thank you, thank you, thank you," the man choked as they loaded the furniture onto the back of his rusty truck and slowly drove away. I watched them disappear around the corner, and I was choked up myself.

As calls started coming in from people responding to our newspaper ad, I joyfully explained, "I'm sorry, the furniture is already gone."

I smiled, confident the furniture was exactly where it should be and proud of my decision.

With clean hands and a pure heart,
may I be worthy to do the work of angels.

ANGELS ALL AROUND US

Recognizing the presence of angels around you may make you feel like you've walked from the shadows into the warmth of sunshine. Suddenly, you feel the nourishment that comes from someone taking the time to look out for you and you alone.

❧◦❧

CHRISTMAS JOY

Anyone who has ever struggled to start a new business can probably appreciate our family's financial situation during the Christmas season of 1960. My husband, Chester, was operating a fledgling appliance-repair service out of our home. During the cold months of winter, there were, of course, no air conditioners to fix and only a few refrigerators needing attention. Business was sagging.

At that time, in addition to our own eight children, we had two families from out of town staying with us. The first family was that of a friend whose husband had died the previous year. She had come with her eight children from Stilwell, Oklahoma, hoping to find a job. The second family had arrived unexpectedly from California: Chester's brother, his wife, and their three children. They remained our guests while Chester's brother also looked for work. A total of 24 people were living together in our six-room home as Christmas drew near!

As the reality set in that we would have no money for presents—or even for a tree—we took the children aside and explained that we would be having a different kind of Christmas this year. We told them that although we would not be buying presents, they could make gifts for one another. Christmas dinner would also be unconventional: beans and cornbread. As we searched their faces for a response, they all agreed that this arrangement was OK with them. They liked beans, they said. I could have kissed each and every one of them right there.

I prepared for the holiday as best I could. I made rag dolls for the small children, but I had nothing for the older ones. I used strips of newspaper and flour-and-water glue to fashion a papier-mâché nativity, which I painted and put on display.

Then, just before his winter break, our ten-year-old son Larry came home from school with some wonderful news. His homeroom teacher had told him that on the last day of classes he could take home the Christmas tree that was standing in the classroom. We were all thrilled, and we anticipated the day when Larry would bring the tree home. But when the day arrived, Larry walked through the door empty-handed. He was met with stares of shock and disappointment.

"Larry! Where's the tree?" we all asked in unison.

Larry explained that a boy in his class had lost his father just a few days earlier, and his family wasn't going to have a Christmas tree that year. So Larry had given the tree to his classmate. Hearing this, we were moved by what Larry had done, and we were proud of his generous spirit.

Then, seizing the moment as an opportunity to teach the younger children, our oldest son, a 17-year-old, reminded them of how fortunate and blessed we all were to have one another, to have our health, to have love, and to have the nativity that Mom had made, which told the real story of Christmas. Christmas was about Jesus, he said, not just about Christmas trees and presents.

With this pep talk, the children got busy making paper stars and snowflakes. Ideas for gifts began to emerge. One of the girls asked if she could give Grandma a small bottle of toilet water she was saving for special occasions. She had only used it a couple times, she said.

Smiling, I said, "Of course! If it's from your heart, it's a wonderful present."

"It's snowing!" the children announced excitedly. They ran to look out the kitchen window, and as I joined them to watch, I saw the beautiful, soft flakes falling noiselessly onto the windowpane. Right then, I said a silent thank-you to God for a warm, dry home and the potato soup that was steaming on the stove. I realized it was a miracle that the kettle had never run out of food, no matter how many people had eaten from it in the last two months.

Just then, the phone rang. "A-1 Appliance Repair," I answered.

The woman's voice on the other end of the line gave the name of a business and wanted to know if Chester could come to the store's location. Then she continued, "Someone told me you were in an accident and broke your leg. How are you?"

I told her that although I had been in an accident the previous week, no one had been injured. "The truck that ran into me had no insurance, and our car was smashed up, but everyone was OK, thank God."

There was a long pause at the other end of the line before the woman said, "Oh! Well, we always make up a food box to help someone who is laid up or who needs it. We thought you were hurt and needed a little help." There was another pause. "Would we hurt your feelings if we offered it to you?"

I thanked her and told her that we would appreciate their gift.

Then she asked, "Do you have your tree up yet?"

When I told her we wouldn't be having one this year, she answered, "Well, we have a big one here. It would be a shame to leave it in an empty store over Christmas."

Instructing us to take the tree along with all the decorations on it, she added, "We heard you have a big family of four or five children."

"Yes, eight!" I said. "This is great! Just great! Thank you so much!" and I hung up the phone.

As Chester got into the pickup with our two oldest sons, I lamented, "I didn't even tell her Merry Christmas!" Chester assured me that he would tell her.

They returned with the most beautiful tree I had ever seen.

"Look! Look! Mama, how pretty!" The children jumped up and down gleefully.

Following the tree came four big boxes of groceries and a huge turkey. One of the children noticed my reaction and said, "Mama, don't cry."

"They're happy tears," I assured her, managing a smile.

The phone rang again. It was the same lady. I thanked her for everything, but she said she had forgotten to give Chester some door prizes that hadn't been claimed. Also, there was a box of clothing that the store next door wanted to give us. She asked to please send Chester right away if we would like to have them. She and the others at the store were ready to close up and go home for the holiday, but they would wait for us to come.

When Chester returned home the second time, he had boxes and boxes of clothes of all sizes for all the children. Other boxes contained electric frying pans, grills, coffeepots, and other small appliances. We gave the most expensive gifts to grandparents and aunts. There was also a big box of piggy banks, enough for us to give one to each of the children who attended our church.

What a wonderful Christmas we had that lean year of 1960. The amazing thing to me is that we didn't even ask God for it, yet he still provided. We certainly thanked him, though—thanked him for speaking softly to folks who could give, and who did give.

We named our ninth and last child Joy, in remembrance of all the joy God has given us.

Which night star is your window light?

On which rainbow do you slide?

Which soft cloud is your playground?

And in which mortal helper do you hide?

STICKS AND STONES

"Sticks and stones may break my bones,
but words can never hurt me."

Once upon a time, my friend Joan believed that childhood chant. At least, she tried to. When she was young. And plump. And constantly being teased. Then things changed. Joan grew up—and out.

As an adult, she tips the scales at well over 500 pounds. Her friends politely say she's heavy. Her doctor writes "morbidly obese" on her chart. The rest of the world calls her fat.

Some people whisper the word. Some people say it out loud, to her face. And, believe it or not, some people say things even worse.

Don't think she hasn't heard the comments. She has, and they hurt. Deeply. But Joan has learned how to avoid the cutting remarks: She simply avoids the people who make them. She stays home.

In her house.

Where it's safe.

But with their 25th wedding anniversary approaching, her husband wanted to do something special for Joan. He planned a magical evening out for the two of them. He made dinner reservations at a nice restaurant and ordered tickets to a show Joan had read about but never thought she would leave her house to see. Knowing it would be difficult to convince Joan to go out, Dan began a persuasive campaign to get her to agree. She finally gave in, reluctantly.

To distract herself from fretting about the impending event, Joan, an accomplished seamstress, decided to sew a dressy new blouse for their celebration. She chose the perfect pattern, the perfect fabric, and busied herself with the project. The more she sewed, the more she wondered if she had made the right decision.

All too soon the big night arrived.

At the restaurant, Joan managed to ignore most of the blunt comments as she made her way across the room to the romantic corner table Dan had reserved. She even managed to disregard the rude stares. But she couldn't overlook the young girl at the table across from them. The youngster never took her eyes off Joan. When the girl headed toward their table, Joan cringed. Experience had taught her that kids could be especially cruel.

The wide-eyed little girl paused next to Joan. Reaching out a single finger, she touched Joan's indigo velvet blouse.

"You're soft and cuddly, like my bunny," she said.

Joan held her breath while a tiny hand gently stroked her sleeve.

"You're so pretty in that shirt." The little girl smiled and walked back to her seat.

A simple comment. A single compliment. That was all. But, according to Joan, it was enough to change her life and to alter her perspective.

"Now," Joan says, "when people stare—and they do stare, believe me—I immediately recall miniature angel fingers caressing my arm. And I'm certain everyone is merely admiring my outfit."

"Now," Joan says, "when people mutter under their breath when I walk by, why, I swear I can hear a young angel's voice reminding me that I'm pretty. And I'm equally sure the words everyone is whispering are compliments."

"That's all I hear—now," Joan says, "only compliments. Words that can never hurt me."

An angel's song on a lonely night
is like a sweet friend's voice.

ONE LESS LOAD

I hadn't even noticed my clothes until then. They definitely had the "slept-in look." But then, they had been slept in! Ever since we'd brought our baby, Lisa, to Children's Hospital, either Frank or I had been by her bedside. The hospital staff had encouraged us to take advantage of the Ronald McDonald house, but that seemed too far away from her hospital bed. It was even hard for me to leave Lisa alone long enough to go to the bathroom. Only now, with her condition stabilized, did I allow myself to think of the world outside the hospital and of my home and family.

How lucky we are to have caring friends and thoughtful neighbors. They had brought in meals and cared for our four other children. And there had been lots of other people who had promised help if we needed it.

Looking at my skirt, I was reminded that I hadn't done the wash for days. The kids had surely run out of clothes. Whatever the teachers must be thinking of our two school-age children, I certainly didn't want to imagine. Though Mike, eight years old, was probably delighted that he hadn't had to change for two weeks!

I can go home for a few hours, I thought, and do the wash. The doctors had assured us that Lisa was out of danger. She probably wouldn't wake until morning, and Frank was asleep in the waiting room. I knew the nurses would wake him if she did begin to fuss.

I walked through the frigid January darkness to our car. My breath fogged the windows. I turned on the defroster to clear them. My mind cleared, too. For the first time, I could look back on the last weeks and think about all that had happened.

As I drove the two hours to our home outside Denver, I recalled rushing our ashen baby to Children's Hospital after our local doctor diagnosed heart failure. The heart specialist said that without surgery Lisa would die. And surgery was risky. She was so tiny, only 13 pounds at 6 months, and her condition was so unstable. The medical team opted to wait a few days, hoping to strengthen her before putting her under anesthesia.

We signed the papers okaying the surgery scheduled three days later, both of us trying to ignore the pessimistic survival statistics. We waited. The doctors wanted Lisa kept quiet because movement and activity made her heart work harder. All the action at home, they said, was what had put her heart into overload. It had been exhausting keeping her entertained while curtailing her movement. We tried to get her to eat more and drink less because sucking her bottle took too much energy. She'd cry in frustration and exhaustion after only an ounce or two. Ice cream was our salvation. We spoon-fed her frozen formula every two to three hours while we waited for the surgery.

As I turned off the highway, my reverie continued. I allowed myself to think back to the most frightening day of all. It was the day before the doctors planned to operate. I was rocking Lisa while the late afternoon sunshine streamed into the room. Suddenly I realized something was dreadfully wrong. Her little lips were turning blue. Frantic, I paged the nurse. She gasped when she saw Lisa. Doctors and nurses rushed in. The surgery could not be postponed. They wheeled her away.

Frank and I sat alone in fear as we waited out the six-hour surgery. We stood up, side by side, when we saw the green-clad surgeon striding into the ICU waiting room. He did not smile reassuringly. They had been able to close the hole in Lisa's heart, but she still might not pull through. The next few hours would tell. They'd keep her in the recovery room so they could constantly monitor her vital signs. We watched the clock and waited. After what seemed an eternity, a volunteer came to tell us they had moved Lisa upstairs, where she was sleeping comfortably.

How we rejoiced! And now, finally, in a few days we would be traveling this very road to bring our baby back home. Then perhaps our lives could return to normal. Then maybe I wouldn't be driving home in the middle of the night to do the wash.

I parked in front of the garage. I'd given up control so completely that I had no idea who was there with the kids, but I didn't want them to be startled by the sound of the garage door opening. Whatever possessed me to come home at this hour, I wondered, as I tiptoed into the dark house. I switched on the light in the dining room. A pile of mail lay on the table, awaiting a neighbor who worked in Denver. He dropped it off at the hospital each day. Beside the mail I saw an amazing sight: stacks of clean, folded clothes. On top of one pile was this poem, signed by a kindly neighbor.

> *I used to say to folks like you,*
> *"Please let me know what I can do.*
> *I'd like to help, I really would,*
> *If you'd just tell me how I could."*
> *But then I began to see that*
> *chances to help were passing me.*
> *So now I try to do small things…*
> *perhaps they'll help me earn my wings.*

I put away the folded clothes but not the poem. Instead, I posted it on my kitchen bulletin board. Before Lisa's surgery I had been a person who said, "Just let me know how I can help." From now on I would not wait to be told.

We stand as tall as angels when we kneel to help a friend.

NICHOLAS

*M*y son Nicholas has always had a soft heart. It's the thing I love best about him. At 13, he is now struggling with the "macho" role society expects of him despite having a tender heart that still wants to save every homeless person and rescue each stray kitten. I am proud that he has remained a compassionate and kind person, even though the teenage years have struck. One of my proudest moments was when he decided to give Christmas to a family in our neighborhood.

Chad and Derek Williams are two boys who attend Nick's junior high. Junior high is painful enough for anyone, but for Chad and Derek it is a daily nightmare. They live alone with their mother, and they are the smallest boys in junior high. The boys are picked on constantly for one thing or another, but a major cause of the taunting is that they wear the same worn, outdated clothes to school every day. Their mother is a loving, hardworking woman, but she is a single mom living on an extremely tight budget, and there is rarely enough money left over for clothes.

Nick has always been sensitive to the pain of others. While many teenage kids wouldn't have even noticed, Nick immediately understood their embarrassment. He appointed himself secret protector to Chad and Derek, and they quickly became the subject of his prayers and worries.

Every year at Christmas our family selects a family and becomes their "Secret Santa." Last year, Nick persuaded us to choose Chad and Derek's family. It's our tradition to provide the makings of a Christmas dinner, as well as to give carefully selected gifts for the family. Nick wanted to buy the boys clothes—but not just any clothes. They had to be "cool"; they had to be "in" clothes. At my ripe old age of 37, I was not qualified to know what was "in." Nick was determined to give Chad and Derek clothes that would stop the taunting and make them feel good about what they wore to school. To many, that may seem trivial, but to a young teenager, it is everything. Whether he realized it or not, Nick wanted to give the boys self-esteem, a chance to fit in. That's quite a gift for a 13-year-old to give.

As we spent endless hours looking for just the right outfits for the boys, I reflected on their mother. I knew a little about what she must be feeling and sacrificing. I remembered the days of my own single motherhood, when every little "extra" went to my children's needs. It had probably been a long time since she had done anything nice for herself. Leaving the kids in the boys' clothing department, I took a quick detour to the bath aisle. Smiling to myself, I selected a bath basket filled to the brim with bath salts, soaps, lotions, loofahs, and all kinds of "take me away" things only a mom can appreciate. I found myself catching Nicholas's spirit. Not knowing the boys' mother well, I searched the store for other gifts that would give her a lift. I looked at clothes, makeup, jewelry, books. I finally selected a book of uplifting stories for moms and a box of truffles.

Delighted, I couldn't wait to show everyone. The spirit of Christmas filled my heart and overflowed into a joyous, childlike feeling of giddiness.

Returning to my children, I found they had finally settled on several articles of clothing. Guessing the boys' sizes was difficult, but we did our best. Nick suddenly remembered the boys wore only old, worn coats to school. And Utah winters demanded good, warm gloves. We chose the thickest, warmest, "coolest" gloves in the store, and I didn't even look at the price tag! We were all grinning with the sheer joy of giving.

We then picked up a family video, two great books, and the Christmas dinner: a fat turkey, all the trimmings, dessert, and candy for the boys' stockings. We couldn't wait to deliver our packages.

Our cart overflowing, we headed for the checkout line. At first worried about spending too much, I was now filled with a sense of peace. As blessed as we were, we ought to share those blessings with others. Standing in line, the thought came to me that while they would appreciate all of these gifts, what would undoubtedly help them even more was money. Next to the counter was a display rack filled with store gift cards. I looked at the amounts and said a quick prayer for guidance. I reached for the $50 card, but my hand picked up the $100 card instead. Praying again, I knew this was right, and I laid the card on top of my purchases. I made a quick call to my husband to make sure this was not too much, and he surprised me with his assurance to go ahead.

I looked at Nicholas as his eyes fell on the gift card, and I laughed as he wheeled around in shock. "Is that for them?" he asked me. I nodded, and my eyes filled with tears as he threw his arms around me and thanked me. What an amazing kid I have.

That night, we wrapped the presents and delivered the huge box to the Williams's doorstep. Nick rang the bell, and then we all ran giggling down the street. The feeling of joy stayed with us long past that night. And it returned the day school resumed. Nick ran all the way home from school to tell me that Derek and Chad had worn their new outfits to school. The clothes fit, and, boy, did they look cool!

The planning and executing of our Secret Santa surprise was the greatest gift our family got that Christmas, and I saw a side of my son that would make any mother weep.

Teenage angels are hard to find these days.

**Some may see angels as choirs in robes
with gold on their heads and rainbows in their wings.
More likely though, they are like caring onlookers,
watching and laughing with pure delight.**

Not So Penny Ante

*T*o the junior high students in the Sunday school class at Grace Methodist Church, the news stories about people starving to death on city streets didn't hit home. In their privileged, suburban world of sack lunches packed from full refrigerators; fast-food burgers, fries, and shakes; and any kind of snack they wanted whenever they wanted it, the problem just didn't make sense.

"If they're hungry, why don't people just go get some food?" one little girl wondered.

"Because they don't have enough money," teacher Sarah Edwards explained.

"Why don't we give them some of our money?" several children wondered.

That was exactly what Sarah had in mind—a project that would encourage the children to count their own blessings and help out other people at the same time. She suggested they earn money doing extra chores at home.

"We can't earn much money. What good can a few dollars do?" one boy asked. "My dad says a dollar isn't good for anything anymore."

But Sarah persisted, and the kids went along. "You'll be surprised at how it all adds up," Sarah promised them.

The children agreed to contribute their allowances, and they all said they would pitch in at home to earn more money. Seeing who had worked the hardest over the week to earn the highest contribution became an anticipated Sunday morning game. After the kids counted up the ante, Sarah collected all the coins and bills and stored them in a manila envelope for safekeeping.

The class goal was to collect at least two hundred dollars for a nearby homeless shelter.

Sarah read passages aloud to the entire class about how Jesus helped the poor, and she used their fund-raising project to illustrate a few lessons about the problems facing the less fortunate. One day, she asked each student to copy down the price of their favorite food at the grocery store, then write it on the blackboard.

"You brought in 50 cents today. How long did you work to earn that?" she asked one boy.

"About an hour," the boy sighed. "I swept the whole driveway, but then I had to do it again because my dad said it wasn't good enough."

"What could you buy with that amount?"

The boy scanned the list and shrugged, not finding a single item he could afford.

Another girl boasted to the class that she had watched her neighbor's dog for the whole day and earned five dollars.

But when she searched the list and realized that five dollars wouldn't buy quite as much as she thought it would, her face fell.

After weeks of work, the kids were inching toward their goal. Sarah decided to let the children help count the money during the next class. But on Friday, when she went to pull the battered manila envelope from the stack of books and papers on the backseat of her car, it was gone. She frantically made a mental list of where she'd been all week: the grocery store, the coffee shop, the gas station, the post office. The envelope could be anywhere! Anyone could have found it, she concluded in dismay, trying to swallow the lump in her throat. Sarah was sick with despair.

She called the local newspaper and asked the editor to print a lost-and-found ad in the Saturday edition. "I wouldn't be too optimistic about getting back an unmarked envelope full of money," the editor said sympathetically.

Sarah knew he was right, but she didn't want to hear it from him, sympathetic or not.

She dreaded facing her students, and she even considered trying to replace the money herself—but she knew it would be too big a stretch on her income. She struggled to figure out how to explain the situation to the children.

When she faced the class on Sunday morning, however, and haltingly told them the bad news, their reaction took her by surprise.

"Don't worry, Mrs. Edwards," one little girl reassured her. "Anyone can make a mistake." The children voted unanimously to start the collection all over again.

Sarah's eyes welled up, and she threw her arms around the two children closest to her. She had never been so proud of her students. Looking into their forgiving faces and eager eyes, she realized that they had heard her lessons and had taken them to heart.

At the end of class, just as they were packing up to leave, the newspaper editor showed up at the door. "I can't believe it," he blurted. "A guy stopped by the office and said he found this in the parking lot at the dry cleaners. He didn't even leave his name—just said he thought it was great what you kids were trying to do." The editor held out the tattered manila envelope.

The children cheered.

"The cleaners!" Sarah gasped. She must have dragged the envelope out along with a bundle of clothes.

Then the editor produced another envelope, this one new and crisp. "And look what else I've got! People have been stopping by the office since yesterday, wanting to help replace your money."

With shaking hands, Sarah opened it up and hastily counted the bills. The envelope contained almost five hundred dollars! The children cheered again, even louder this time. Sarah breathed a quiet "Thank you."

The next week, Sarah and the class took a trip to the homeless shelter. The kids were so excited they could hardly sit still. They made speeches, read a poem they had prepared, and sang songs. Before stepping forward to present the money, the youngest child reached for Sarah's hand. Together they handed the shelter director their gift.

"Thank you all," the director smiled. "This will buy a lot of food for our shelter. You've done a wonderful thing."

The students beamed with pride.

At class the next week, as Sarah and the children talked excitedly about the experience, Sarah concluded, "I think we all learned something from this. Never doubt that your individual efforts can make a difference—and never, ever give up hope!"

**For God so loves us, his children,
that he sent a heavenly host of angels
to guide, protect, and inspire us.**

WAKE-UP CALL

*I*t wasn't uncommon for me to go by the supermarket bakery on my way to work to grab a fresh donut and a cup of coffee. Being single and usually in a hurry, eating out was the rule for me rather than the exception.

On this particular day as I walked into the bakery, I noticed a young woman (she looked to be in her early thirties) sitting alone at a table. She appeared to have just crawled out of bed after sleeping in her clothes all night. Tattered grocery bags were scattered around her feet. These were not bags filled with groceries from the market but rather with what appeared to be all her earthly possessions.

I felt empathy for her but quickly brushed it out of my mind. I didn't have time to concern myself with a stranger.

After purchasing my donut and coffee, I glanced at the clock. I had 15 minutes to eat, drink, and drive the remaining five miles to work. I was right on time.

From where I was seated, I could see the mystery woman. She had nothing to eat or drink on her table, and for a fleeting second, I thought it might be "a nice thing to do" to buy her some breakfast.

I immediately dismissed the thought. After all, this was the big city, and the sight of a street person was not uncommon.

And I, a young executive-type, was in a hurry. Besides, I told myself, people are just asking for trouble by approaching strangers.

I pushed her out of my head.

Right on schedule, I finished my breakfast and got up. Passing the woman, I could not help but notice how forlorn she looked sitting there, staring off into space.

I wonder if she's hungry. She's probably a street person. Looks as though she's had that same dress on for a week. No telling how long it's been since she's had a bath, I thought. *But she's one of God's own, just like me.* The notion gave me pause, but I kept on walking.

As I approached my car, the voice inside me said: *Go give that woman some money.* I was already 50 feet from the bakery. It was too late. I got in my car and headed for work.

As I drove into the parking lot a couple minutes later, I was again prompted by the voice: *I want you to go give that woman some money.*

This time, the voice was more commanding than requesting. Commanding enough that I had to stop what I was doing and pay attention.

Okay, I thought, *but I really have to hurry.*

I drove back to the store. Before I got out of the car, I pulled out my wallet and looked inside. Two twenties and a five. I pulled out a twenty, rolled it neatly in the palm of my hand, and walked back into the store.

The woman was still there, head in her hands, elbows on the table, with her face now totally hidden from view.

"Excuse me," I said. She either didn't hear me or chose to ignore me.

"Excuse me," I repeated. She looked up as if to say, "What do you want?"

I placed the money on the corner of her table.

"What's this?" she asked angrily.

I was shocked and couldn't think of anything to say.

"Well, what is it? What do you want?"

I recovered quickly. "I'm sorry if I offended you..., I...I'm just...here you go."

I thought she was going to throw it in my face.

Not knowing what else to do, I turned to make a hasty retreat from the store. I glanced back and saw that she was hurrying to put on her shoes and follow me. I kept walking as fast as I could.

"Hey!" she yelled.

Briskly, I exited the store and began crossing the parking lot as quickly as I could.

"Hey, you!" I heard again. This time she was outside.

I stopped in my tracks, assuming a defensive posture. I had no idea what to expect from her, but I was sure it would be some kind of attack.

"You gotta know this," she said as she came closer.

In retrospect, I'm amused at how I reacted to her approach. I pulled one arm up to my chest, ready to fend off any sudden blows, threw my head back, and firmly planted my feet. I was ready for anything.

"My mother died last week," she began, starting to cry. "I couldn't even afford to call home, much less go . . ."

I began to relax my guard.

". . . and this morning, I didn't even have enough money to buy food . . . ,"

My heart went out to her.

". . . not even a donut . . . ."

I couldn't help feeling the fullness within myself, remembering how hungry I'd been just half an hour ago.

"I was sitting there, being really angry with God, and I told him, 'Why can't you take care of me the way you take care of other folks?' I was really mad. And about that time you come up with that little do-gooder smile on your face and say, 'Excuse me, excuse me.'

"And then I saw that money," she said, softening her tone, smiling a little. "That's a lot of money for me."

She began to cry again. "Well, I know now that God does take care of me. . . . He always has. . . . And I want to apologize . . . to you and to him."

"And now," she said, taking a deep breath and smiling, "I'm gonna go have breakfast."

I got in my car, started it, adjusted the controls, and began to review the events of the morning. I had to stay in the parking lot for a few minutes. I couldn't see to drive because of the tears clouding my eyes.

I'd been so busy, I had actually resisted a "call" from God. Fortunately, I listened the second time.

**There isn't a valley low enough that an angel
can't carry you through it.**

THE ENCOURAGER

I don't know his name, but I recognize his face. Each morning we pass each other on the walking trail around the lake where we exercise. He is Japanese, wiry yet spry, in his late sixties or early seventies.

First lap, we smile at each other in recognition and say "good morning" as he walks past me going in the opposite direction.

I use this time to reflect and meditate as well as to keep my body toned and flexible. Years ago I used to jog a couple of miles each morning. Then a car accident hurt my back and legs, and even though I recovered, I couldn't jog again. My knees were too weak, so I began walking instead.

Second lap, the man smiles again and holds up two fingers as he passes.

I wonder about his life. How does he spend his time when he's not here? What draws him to this place? What milestones has he passed in his life? I ponder the lives of other people on the exercise trail, too, wondering if they are happy or burdened, if they use this time to talk to God like I do.

Third lap, the man laughs gently and holds up three fingers as he passes by again.

I used to get up at 5:15 every morning and go to the gym with my husband to work out with weights and machines. But time and life had put an end to that. I ruptured a disc in my neck, and after corrective surgery to remove the disc, I began long, torturous hours of physical therapy. I became depressed and discouraged after months with no improvement; my arm was weak, and I was in constant pain. A nerve had been damaged in my right arm and shoulder, so I could barely carry a gallon of milk, let alone lift weights. I had to quit my job as a bookkeeper and office manager, since using a computer for long periods of time caused swelling and pain. I finally had to admit that my life would need some adjustments. Now I am just starting to get into some new routines.

Fourth lap, we're both breathing a little harder, and our steps seem to be a little slower. But the man smiles as he greets me again with four fingers in the air.

"One more," he cheers as he walks past.

I'm feeling tired and had thought about cutting my walk short and heading home. But I don't want to let the man down. His optimism and enthusiasm encourage me to go one more lap with him. I figure if he can go one more lap at his age, surely I can, too. I pick up my sagging rhythm, lift my head, and walk.

I look at the scenery around me. The lake, surrounded by trees, is serene. Birds are singing and looking for food, colorful flowers are blooming all around, and the morning sun is shining up above. I smile and breathe deeply, filling my lungs with crisp, fresh air.

The man waves as we finish our fifth lap.

"See you tomorrow!" he calls.

I wonder if he realizes how much encouragement he has given me. So often just a smile, a kind word, or a friendly wave is enough to lift my spirits and keep me going. I hope that I can do the same for others who need a little encouragement, too.

"Yes, I'll see you tomorrow!" I call back, already anticipating the next day's walk.

**May you always walk
with the morning star to guide you,
the summer sun on your back,
and an angel by your side.**